Wealthy ever After

PAMELA MAASS GARRETT, J.D.

Wealthy ever After

A PROVEN SYSTEM TO GROW, MULTIPLY, AND PROTECT YOUR WEALTH FOR GENERATIONS

BEST SELLER PUBLISHING

ISBN: 978-1966395423

Disclaimer

The stories included within *Wealthy Ever After* are an amalgamation of past and present clients. Any identifying details have been altered to protect the privacy of their story while keeping the integrity of the situation intact.

The information provided in this book does not, and is not intended to, constitute financial, legal, or tax advice. Instead, this book's information, content, and materials are for general informational purposes only. Information in this book may not constitute the most up-to-date financial, legal, tax, or other relevant information.

This book contains links to third-party websites. These links are provided for the reader's convenience; the author does not endorse the contents of any third-party sites.

Readers of this book should consult with a financial advisor, attorney, or tax professional regarding any financial, legal, or tax matter. No reader should act or refrain from acting based on the information contained herein without first seeking personalized professional advice. Only your advisors can assure that the information contained herein—and your interpretation of it—applies to your situation.

Use of, and access to, this book or any of the links or resources contained within do not create an attorney-client, financial advisor-client, or tax professional-client relationship between the reader and the author, contributors, or affiliated organizations.

The views expressed in this book are those of the author in their capacity and do not represent the views of any affiliated organizations or employers. All liability concerning actions taken or not taken based on the contents of this book is expressly disclaimed. The content is provided "as is," with no representations that it is error-free or comprehensive.

For more information, please contact:
Best Seller Publishing®
1775 US-1 #1070
St. Augustine, FL 32084
or call 1 (626) 765-9750
Visit us online at: www.BestSellerPublishing.org

FOR MY HUSBAND, MY DAUGHTER, AND
MY SON—MY GREATEST LOVE STORY
AND MY HAPPILY EVER AFTER.

CONTENTS

INTRODUCTION:
YOUR WEALTH STORY STARTS HERE

How I Went from Money Stress to Money Clarity
(And You Can Too!)

I once believed financial stress was just a part of life, like never-ending laundry or an inbox that keeps growing. Bills, unexpected expenses, that random $14.99 subscription I thought I had canceled, it seemed like a never-ending game of financial whack-a-mole. I told myself: "If I can make more money, everything will be fine."

I started my own business, thinking I had finally cracked the code. But instead of relief, starting a business brought a whole new level of financial anxiety. I wasn't just managing my expenses anymore. Now, I had:

- Payroll for my team
- Overwhelming taxes that felt like a heavy weight, draining my savings faster than I could keep up
- Business expenses that turned my bank account into a revolving door, money barely stopped before spinning right back out

Making money wasn't the main issue, managing money was.

THE TURNING POINT

As an estate planning attorney, I have worked with CEOs, doctors, and business owners, people who looked prosperous on paper. Behind the scenes, however, many of them were just one financial setback away from disaster.

They were not broke, but they also weren't financially free. Some were troubled by possible problems, not enjoying life as much as they'd hoped.

I saw patterns:

- Some people had high incomes but little or no savings. They made seven figures but spent money so fast that they felt trapped in a cycle of high earning and high stress.
- Some had assets but no real plan. They had businesses, real estate, and investments, but they had no strategy to protect them from lawsuits, taxes, or disastrous financial decisions.
- And then there were also the truly wealthy, the confident people with money and control.

These truly wealthy families weren't just rich. They were strategic. They had systems to grow, multiply, and protect their wealth.

But it wasn't just their financial strategies that set them apart.

Their mindset was different.

They didn't see money as something to be chased. They saw it as a relationship that needed to be nurtured and safeguarded. Financial success isn't just about how much you earn.

It's about your relationship with money. Is it a balanced, supportive relationship where you work together, or a toxic one where money dictates your choices? The way you engage with money determines whether it empowers you or controls you. Once I shifted my mindset, everything changed for me.

I stopped working harder and started working smarter. I know, it might be a cliché, but...

I stopped seeing money as stressful and started treating it as my greatest ally.

I stopped thinking about wealth as something to achieve and started seeing it as a cycle, a system or a process.

And that's exactly what this book will teach you.

THE WEALTH SHIFT: THE 3 WEALTH ACCELERATORS

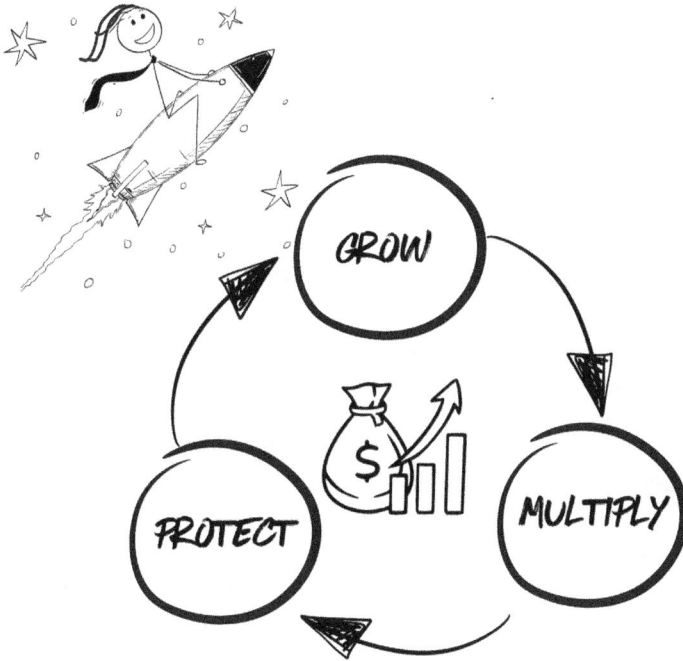

After working with hundreds of wealthy clients, conducting my own research, and applying these principles in my own life, I uncovered a truth that changed everything:

True financial security isn't built once, it's built three times.

Over the years, I studied what the wealthiest families did differently. I saw the same three strategies used repeatedly, by billionaires, dynasties like the Rockefellers, and financially free individuals who had stopped worrying about money. These weren't random tactics or lucky breaks. They were part of a *repeatable system*, a blueprint I call the 3 Wealth Accelerators: Grow, Multiply, Protect.

Most people believe that making more money will set them free, but without a system, they stay stuck in the same cycle of earning and spending. The wealthy don't work harder, they follow this proven 3-phase formula to build, expand, and secure their financial future.

Wealth Accelerator #1: GROW

You start by growing personally, growing control, and growing income, developing a strong money mindset, taking charge of your finances, and building multiple income streams. But without the next step, you're just earning and spending on repeat.

Wealth Accelerator #2: MULTIPLY

To break free from the cycle, you must *multiply your money*, learning how to invest and make your wealth grow on its own. This is where real financial freedom begins. But growth alone isn't enough. Without protection, one setback can wipe everything out.

Wealth Accelerator #3: PROTECT

This is where everything changes. True wealth is built when you protect what you've created, minimizing taxes, securing your assets, and setting up a long-term plan so your money lasts for generations.

This Is Your Turning Point

I saw this pattern not just in my clients' experiences but in my own journey. Like so many others, I once believed that working harder, earning more, or investing smarter would eliminate financial stress. But without a system, more money doesn't solve the problem, it just makes it bigger.

That's why I wrote *Wealthy Ever After*, to give you the blueprint to finally create lasting financial freedom. This book will show you how to Grow, Multiply, and Protect your wealth, so it doesn't just flow into your life, it stays, grows, and supports the legacy you're building.

The 3 Wealth Accelerators changed my life, and they can change yours too.

The Biggest Mistake People Make

Most people get stuck in one phase of the cycle.

- Some never move past growth. They believe working harder is the answer, but they never learn how to multiply their money.
- Others focus only on multiplication. They invest and grow wealth, but without protection, they lose much of it to taxes, lawsuits, or bad financial planning.
- Too many people ignore protection altogether. They build wealth but fail to secure it, leaving their children and grandchildren needing to start from scratch.

If you complete the cycle, you will have achieved true financial freedom. Once you master these three accelerators, your money will work for you, not just for a lifetime, but for generations.

Your Wealthy Ever After Starts Now

Right now, you are building your wealth story.
The question is, where will you stop?

- Will you work hard but never feel like it's enough?
- Will you grow your wealth, only to see it drained by taxes and financial mistakes?
- Or will you create something that lasts, giving you freedom, peace of mind, and a legacy?

The wealthy don't just think differently about money, they use money differently. They follow a system.
And now, that system is yours.
This book will show you how to grow, multiply, and protect your wealth, on repeat.
Not just for now.
Not just for retirement.
But for generations.

FIND YOUR FINANCIAL POWER

I didn't grow up wealthy. I didn't have a family fortune or a trust fund waiting for me. There was no safety net to catch me if I failed. Like most people, I started building my financial future one step at a time, making plenty of mistakes along the way.

Here's what I've done

- I built a seven-figure business while raising a family.
- I've assisted thousands of families in safeguarding their assets and building generational wealth.
- I was invited and was featured on The Drew Barrymore Show as an expert in financial and estate planning.
- I grew my social media audience to 2.8 million followers by making financial literacy clear, simple, and engaging.

Your financial journey is not about my story; it is about yours. My role is not to dictate what you should do, but to provide you with the tools, strategies, and steps that have helped me and many others. True power lies in applying, adapting, and trusting yourself to make the right decisions.

This book isn't about me; it's about empowering you to take charge of your financial future. At the end of the day, the person you need to listen to the most is yourself. You have what it takes to change your life, I'm here to help you unlock your potential.

WHAT THIS BOOK IS

This book is a *toolbox* designed to help you take control of your finances.

It's filled with practical, easy-to-follow steps that anyone can utilize, regardless of their starting point. It empowers you to establish a financial system that fits your life and fosters peace, clarity, and momentum.

Whether you're overwhelmed by bills, managing a comfortable income, or just beginning to contemplate financial goals, this book is crafted to meet you at your current situation and provide actionable strategies to help you progress. It's about achieving true financial freedom, not just in the spreadsheet figures but in how you live your life and spend your time. This roadmap guides you in growing wealth, multiplying it, and protecting it long-term. It's personal, strategic, and, most importantly, achievable.

WHAT THIS BOOK ISN'T

This book isn't a get-rich-quick scheme. If you're looking for shortcuts or promises of overnight wealth, you won't find them here. Financial transformation requires focus, intention, and consistency. It's also not an overly technical financial manual. There's no confusing jargon or one-size-fits-all formulas here. This isn't about becoming an expert in day trading or exploring the intricacies of tax law. Instead, it's about mastering the basics that make a difference, habits, strategies, and systems that work for real people.

Finally, this isn't about telling you what you "should" or "shouldn't" do. It's about providing the tools to trust yourself and make the right decisions for your financial future. This book is yours to explore, a guide, but the hero of this story is you.

A WORD ON ECONOMIC STORMS

Chances are, you might have already endured multiple economic storms. Perhaps you experienced the dot-com crash, the aftermath of the 9/11 attacks, or the economic upheaval caused by the COVID-19 pandemic. These moments were unpredictable, unsettling, and often financially devastating.

Here's the good news: history shows us that we recover from economic storms. Markets rebound, opportunities reemerge, and we find a way to rebuild. The processes and strategies outlined in this book aren't dependent on perfect conditions. They're designed to work during highs and lows, providing stability even when the world feels out of control. This book aims to help you focus on what you can control. By committing to organizing your finances, building proactive systems, and aligning your money with your values, you create a foundation that can weather even the most unpredictable storms.

Economic turbulence happens. Financial clarity and the right strategies ensure you're not at the mercy of things you do not control. By following the path outlined in this book, you'll position yourself to withstand economic uncertainty and thrive in the long run. Regardless of the economic situation, the tools and principles presented here serve as your roadmap to resilience and success.

You can't control the storms, but you can control how you prepare for and respond to them.

With the practices you'll learn here, you'll be prepared to survive and thrive.

THE WEALTH-HEALTH CONNECTION: WHY FIXING YOUR RELATIONSHIP WITH MONEY FIXES EVERYTHING ELSE

Let's discuss the side effects of financial stress:

- Waking up at 3 AM worrying about bills
- A knot in your stomach every time you swipe your card
- The occasional (or not-so-occasional) "I deserve this" shopping spree that just makes things worse

For me, everything changed when I changed my relationship with money.

- I slept better
- I stopped feeling guilty about spending money on things I enjoyed
- I made better decisions for my family and my future

I observed the same thing happen for my clients:

- The entrepreneur who started paying herself first rather than putting everything back into her business
- The doctor who stopped feeling guilty about spending money, and instead started enjoying things she could do with her money, guilt-free and confident
- The CEO who set up a generational wealth plan for his children and grandchildren no longer rationalized that his kids would "figure it out" but gave them a gentle start in their future directions.

Improving your finances isn't merely about accumulating wealth; it involves understanding where your money flows and how it impacts your life. This is precisely what I will demonstrate. Money is more than a survival tool, it is a source of joy, opportunity, and legacy.

Before we proceed, laying the foundation for your financial journey is important.

Clarity fosters confidence.

Too often, people set vague goals regarding wealth, tossing out random numbers without clearly understanding what they truly need to feel financially free. That's where most people get stuck, they lack a roadmap.

This section aims to address that. Instead of waiting for a distant "someday" when everything magically aligns, you'll begin acting immediately. Think of this as your quick win, an effective tool crafted to help you gain clarity on your financial needs and aspirations.

When you finish this exercise, you will know exactly what you are working toward. You will have a personalized roadmap that transforms financial stress into clarity and actionable steps. This is your first step toward creating a life of freedom and abundance.

YOUR FIRST STEP: YOUR PERSONALIZED MONEY ROADMAP

When asked, "How much money do you need to feel financially free?", most people respond casually with a figure, $1 million, $3 million, $10 million, or $100 million.

When you ask, "Okay, what exactly would you do with that money?" they have no idea.

As we delve into this book, I want you to understand what you desire and why.

Step 1: Price Your Dream Life

Take a moment and write down the actual numbers for:

- Your dream home (purchase price or monthly payment)
- Your ideal car
- Your dream vacations each year
- The amount you'd want in reserves (emergency fund, investments)
- Education for your children (private school, college savings)
- Lifestyle expenses (clothing, self-care, fitness, dining out)
- Philanthropy or giving (causes, family support)

Step 2: Look One Year Out

If you can't have everything on the list right now, what would you need in the next 12 months to move closer?

Maybe it's saving for a down payment on a house or paying off a debt, draining your income.

Focus on what's realistic and what would make a meaningful difference.

Step 3: Calculate Your Ballpark Retirement Number

Take your retirement dream lifestyle and determine what it would cost annually.

Multiply that by 25 (a general rule for how much you need invested to retire comfortably).

When I did this exercise, I realized:

- A lot of what I thought I needed was way less expensive than I assumed
- My dream life was within reach much sooner than I expected
- Financial clarity gave me control over my future, no more guessing

GO FURTHER WITH THE LAW MOTHER APP

To make this even easier, download the Law Mother App, where you can:

- Get access to trusted advisors for estate planning, investing, and tax strategies
- Join a community of people on the same wealth journey as you

To get FREE access to the Law Mother App, visit WealthyEver.com/book or scan the QR code below to get started.

Are You Ready to Take Control of Your Financial Future?

By the end of this book, you won't just understand money, you'll control it.

The tools you need are all here. The question is: Will you use them? Let's get started. Your Wealthy Ever After starts now.

PART 1

GROW

1

GROW PERSONALLY – MASTER YOUR MONEY MINDSET

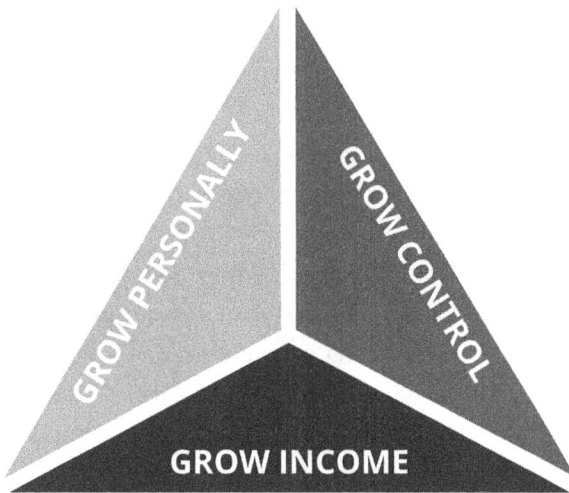

In the introduction, we uncovered a powerful truth, financial success isn't just about how much you earn, but about your relationship with money. That relationship begins in your mind. Before you can grow your wealth, you must grow personally, by mastering your money mindset. And for me, that transformation started the moment I realized fear, not numbers, was running my life.

THE MOMENT I REALIZED MONEY
FEAR WAS RUNNING MY LIFE

I began my business expecting to receive a substantial bonus from my previous employer. That money would provide me with a safety net, assist me in getting things underway, and ease the transition into entrepreneurship, making it less risky.

The bonus didn't arrive. I had already quit my job, and my husband's income wasn't sufficient to cover our expenses. Suddenly, I was facing a very real and quite terrifying financial cliff! That's when I made a decision that felt both bold and reckless: I applied for a zero percent interest credit card and used it to fund my business.

Every morning, limiting thoughts occupied my mind:

You will fail.

This will ruin everything.

You will end up on the streets.

It wasn't only my own thoughts I had to battle. Family members and friends, well-meaning but, feeling deeply worried, shared their fears and doubts: "Are you sure this is a good idea? What if you can't earn enough to support your family? Perhaps you should think about returning to a stable job before it's too late."

Each morning, I had to battle against all of this, my own panic, their doubts, and the fear of making the biggest mistake of my life.

I calmed myself by focusing on the numbers: the simple math, the plan I had in place, and the six months I gave myself to make this work.

Numbers don't create emotions. They are not the source of fear and doubt; our thoughts about them are.

I wasn't focused on mindset shifts or financial strategies at the time; I was merely trying to survive. The first six months were not easy. There were nights when I lay awake, second-guessing everything. The doubts did not completely disappear, and the voices of worry from others still echoed in my mind. But each day, I chose to focus on what I knew rather than what I feared. The numbers remained steady, showing me that I had enough credit to get through this window of time. They reminded me that every dollar spent was not a leap into failure but an investment in something bigger.

I celebrated my small wins every day. The first client I secured gave me a sense of momentum. Weeks turned into months, and by the end of those six months, I had exceeded my earnings goals. My business didn't just survive, it began to thrive. The cliff I initially perceived was never truly there. I built a bridge that carried me to the other side by following the plan.

At the time, I believed that a certain amount of money would shield me from difficult emotions. I thought that if I had more, I wouldn't have to face anxiety or stress. However, we know that isn't true, someone with $500 can experience financial freedom, while someone with $5 million may feel constant worry due to their beliefs about money.

Looking back, I learned that the amount of money in my bank account was never the enemy; my fear was. Numbers are neutral, they don't dictate success or failure. What matters is the narrative you construct about them. When I adjusted my mindset and trusted my plan, I didn't just meet my financial goals, I demonstrated to myself that I could handle anything. And that made all the difference.

WHY I KEPT REPEATING THE SAME MONEY MISTAKES

I earned more money but still felt broke, because I was trapped in outdated money patterns. The mistake wasn't solely my financial choices; it was that I was repeating ingrained beliefs about money. The negative thoughts triggered the same feelings, leading to the same behaviors. Without transforming my beliefs, I continued to repeat the same financial patterns.

Every time I got ahead, I self-sabotaged:

- A surprise expense would wipe out my savings.
- I'd convince myself I "deserved" a splurge, only to regret it later.
- I'd feel guilty for having money,

If you've ever received a raise, only to find yourself still living paycheck to paycheck, you may understand this cycle. More money didn't alleviate my financial stress; it merely provided more room to repeat the same mistakes.

THE HIDDEN MONEY SOFTWARE RUNNING IN THE BACKGROUND OF YOUR BRAIN

Imagine that you downloaded a set of money beliefs into your mind:

- From Your Parents: "We can't afford that."
- From Your Community: "Money is for men to manage."
- From Your Past Experiences: "Money disappears as quickly as it comes."

Some beliefs are useful:

- "Money can create opportunities."

Many beliefs are like outdated software bugs:

- "Making money is hard."
- "Rich people are greedy."
- "I'm just bad with money."
- "More money will solve all my problems."

These beliefs are invisible scripts that shape how you earn, spend, and save, while you remain unaware.

Example: Consider how you feel when an unexpected bill arrives.

If your first reaction is, "Ugh, money seems to disappear as soon as I get it," that's an old script at play. Now, imagine thinking instead, "Good thing I have my opportunity fund."

Same scenario, different script.

HOW WOMEN ARE TAUGHT TO FEAR MONEY

If you are a woman, you have likely received a financial script that differs significantly from those received by men.

Women were not legally permitted to have their own credit cards until 1974.

From an early age, many women are taught to believe:

- "Be careful with money, you never know when it will run out."
- "It's not ladylike to talk about money."
- "You should be grateful for what you have and not ask for more."
- "Rich women are selfish."

These beliefs don't just disappear when we become adults. They appear every time we hesitate to ask for a raise, feel guilty about earning more than our spouse, and undervalue our skills in business.

Example: Have you ever felt the need to justify a financial win?

"I received a big bonus - but I worked so hard for it!"
Did you notice this impulse to justify?
That's a financial script in action.
Instead, you might celebrate the win: "I received a big bonus, and I'm excited!"

BRIDGING THE GAP: REWRITING LIMITING BELIEFS IN STEPS

Rather than jumping straight to an empowering belief, you may need a bridge belief, a belief that your mind can accept as possible.

Step 1: Spot the Limiting Belief

- Example: "Money is hard to make."
- Real-life scenario
  A friend invites you to a luxury vacation, and your first reaction is, "It must be nice. I could never afford that."
  Questions to ask yourself
  » What do I believe about money that might not be true?
  » Where did this belief originate, from my family, culture, or past experiences?
  » How does this belief appear in my life (e.g., decisions, emotions, or habits)?

>> Is this belief helping me or holding me back?

>> What would my life look like if I didn't believe this?

Step 2: Create a Bridge Belief

Shift to a bridge belief your mind can readily accept:

- "Mastering money is a skill I can learn."
- "There are ways to make money that I haven't explored yet."
- Real-life scenario
  Instead of shutting down at the thought of a luxury trip, you say, "How could I afford this trip?"

Step 3: Reinforce It with Evidence

Your brain needs evidence to accept a new belief.

- "I made an extra $100 last month without working extra hours."
- "I've learned other skills before, why wouldn't I be able to learn about money? skills?"
- Example
  Remember the first time you learned to cook or to use a new kitchen tool or app?
  Money management is a skill you can learn, and this book will help you on your way.

Step 4: Install an Empowering Belief

Once your mind accepts the bridge belief, you can upgrade:

- "I'm learning how to manage money" → "I am in control of my finances."
- From "Money is a skill I can learn" to "I attract money and opportunities effortlessly."

SELF-COACHING MODEL

One of the most powerful tools I discovered during my life coaching certification is Brooke Castillo's self-coaching model. This model taught me how our experiences and results are deeply intertwined with our thoughts, and how we can change both by taking control of our mental narrative. It's simple, logical, and incredibly effective. You can use the model to gain awareness of your patterns. Once you recognize the cycle, you can interrupt it and choose a new response.

The model is comprised of five components that collaborate to form a loop:

Circumstances

These are the factual, neutral events occurring in your life. They represent situations beyond your control. For example: Circumstance: Amount of money owed on a credit card.

Thoughts

These are your interpretations of circumstances as perceived by your brain. For example, thought: I am irresponsible with money.

Feelings

Your thoughts create emotions. For example, emotion: Shame

Actions

Your feelings drive behaviors; they're what you do or don't do. Ex. Action: Charge more to the credit card, avoid looking at finances, blame external factors

Results

The outcome of your actions always connects to the thoughts that started the loop. Ex. Result: Don't take responsibility for finances, cycle repeats.

The best part? Changing your thoughts can shift your entire experience, your feelings, actions, and the results you create.

How the Model Works

Let's break this down with a practical example.

Scenario

You have an unexpected bill for $400 sitting on your desk.

Circumstances (Neutral Facts)

You received a bill for $400.

Note that a circumstance is neutral. It doesn't carry emotion, it's a fact. The bill exists; that's all.

Thoughts (Your Interpretation)

When you examine the bill, your mind reflects, *"I'll never get ahead. There's always another expense."*

Feelings (Emotions Created by Your Thoughts)

This thought may trigger feelings of hopelessness, stress, or frustration.

Actions (What You Do or Don't Do Because of Your Feelings)

Feeling overwhelmed, you may avoid opening the bill and procrastinate on addressing it. or vent to a friend about how unfair life is.

Results (Outcomes Created by Your Actions)

By avoiding the bill, you incur late fees and harm your credit. And guess what? This reinforces the belief *"I'll never get ahead."* It becomes a cycle.

EXERCISE: HOW YOU CAN SELF-COACH

To self-coach, you use the model to interrupt the cycle. Here's how you do it step by step:

A. Identify Your Current Thought Model

Start by writing down the circumstance, your thoughts, feelings, actions, and results. Ask yourself, "What am I thinking that's creating this result?"
Example (continuing from above):

- Circumstance: The $400 bill.
- Thought: *"I'll never get ahead."*
- Feeling: Hopelessness.
- Action: Avoid opening the bill.
- Result: Late fees.

B. Challenge Your Thought

Once you've identified your original thought, ask yourself some questions:

- Is this thought true?
- Is there another way to think about this?
- How does this thought make me feel?
- Is this thought helping me create the result I want?

Example: Instead of automatically believing, *"I'll never get ahead,"* try challenging this thought by asking, *"What can I do to stay on top of this bill?"* or, *"What steps can I take to feel more in control next month?"*

C. Choose a More Empowering Thought

After challenging your thought, you can choose to reframe it. You don't need to leap to extreme positivity, just shift to a bridge thought that you can believe in.

Example:

Maybe instead of "I'll never get ahead," consider thinking, "Paying this bill will bring me peace of mind," or even something as simple as, "I can handle this."

D. Connect Your New Thought to a Feeling

Notice how changing your thought shifts your emotional state. A thought like *"I can handle this"* might create a feeling of empowerment or calm instead of hopelessness.

E. Take Purposeful Action

Since you feel calm, you might take different actions, such as pulling out the bill, reviewing your budget, or planning to pay it off in installments.

F. Create a New Result

The new action results in no late fees, no added anxiety, and a growing sense of control over your finances.

Real-Life Application

Here's another example, this time with a career challenge.

Example Scenario:

You didn't get the promotion you wanted.

- » Circumstance: You applied for a promotion and didn't get it.
- » Thought (Old Belief): *"I must not be good enough for the role."*
- » Feeling: Defeated.
- » Action: You stop applying for promotions or avoid feedback from your boss.
- » Result: You stay in the same position, reinforcing the thought *"I'm not good enough."*

To self-coach, you would follow the same steps:

> » Identify your circumstances and current thoughts.
> » Challenge the thought. Ask yourself, *"Is this the only explanation? Could there be another reason for not receiving the promotion?"*
> » Replace the thought with something more helpful, like, *"I can learn from this experience and try again."*
> » Generate a new feeling, such as determination or curiosity.

- You can undertake various actions, such as scheduling a meeting to request feedback from your manager or focusing on specific skills to enhance your application for next time.
- Develop a new outcome, such as a more defined career plan or an improved likelihood of success in the future.

Practicing Self-Coaching Weekly

The beauty of the Self-Coaching Model is that it can be applied to any area of life, money, relationships, health, career, and more. Whenever you feel stuck, overwhelmed, or not where you want to be, you can pause and ask yourself:

- What am I thinking?
- How is this thought influencing my current results?
- What other options might I explore to achieve a different outcome?

Remember, changing your thoughts doesn't mean ignoring reality. It involves recognizing that many of your interpretations are merely optional stories your mind has chosen to accept. While you can't control every circumstance in your life, you can control how you think, feel, and act.

Regularly practicing this process will help you transition from disempowered thinking to empowerment, allowing you to create the results you truly desire in your life. This embodies the power of self-coaching.

MONEY AS A RELATIONSHIP

Have you ever thought about your relationship with money as if it were a friendship? Picture money as your closest friend. Like any strong relationship, it requires attention, care, and respect. If you consistently ignore or mistreat a friend, the relationship becomes strained. However, the bond thrives when you show gratitude, support them, and build trust.

The same goes for money.

Like any relationship, your financial relationship flourishes based on your focus. If you concentrate on what's working, you'll cultivate more of it. If you linger in scarcity, you'll reinforce a feeling of scarcity. The more respect and care you show towards your money, the more it will reciprocate by "showing up" for you.

WHAT HAPPENS WHEN YOU IGNORE MONEY?

Consider a friend you no longer call, text, or avoid altogether. Over time, that friendship begins to fade. Miscommunication occurs, and you start to feel distant. Similarly, neglecting finances can lead to chaos.

When you ignore your finances, whether by avoiding your bank balance, refusing to plan, or neglecting to check credit card statements, money begins to feel like a source of stress. Much like neglected friendships, overlooked finances can become messy and unpredictable.

Example

If you habitually swipe your credit card without checking your balance, you may avoid confronting your finances until the bill arrives. By that time, the "friendship" has already fostered resentment, you're now facing interest charges, late fees, or other surprises.

When you turn a blind eye to money, it often feels like it's disappearing faster than you can earn it. You lose control, and in that state of avoidance, important financial goals feel out of reach.

What Happens When You Pay Attention to Money?

Now, consider a best friend with whom you frequently connect. You make time for them, actively listen, and express gratitude for their importance in your life. That friendship flourishes because you demonstrate effort. Trust builds, the connection deepens, and the rewards are mutual.

When you consistently pay attention to money, your relationship with it improves. Treat money like your best friend:

- Check in regularly: This might mean reviewing your accounts once a week
- Speak truthfully: Be straightforward about your goals and ensure your spending aligns with them.
- Show gratitude: Appreciate what money brings to your life, even for small things like a meal or a home.

THE REWARD OF RESPECTING MONEY

The irony is that when we stop viewing money as a stressful problem and start seeing it as a valued partner, it shows up for us. It begins to feel stable, reliable, and even supportive.

You can feel more at ease knowing where your money is going. You can plan for the future with enthusiasm instead of anxiety. As this relationship deepens, money becomes a tool you use to create the vibrant life you envision.

Remember, your relationship with money isn't about perfection; it's about consistency. Like the best friend who doesn't mind if you call at 8 a.m. on a Sunday or share a quiet cup of coffee on a rainy afternoon, money seeks connection. When you treat it as a trusted ally, it supports your growth in return.

FEELINGS AS FUEL

When it comes to money, logic isn't always in charge, our emotions often take control. Consider this: every financial decision we make, from saving to spending, is influenced by how we *feel*. That's why understanding the role of emotions in financial choices is so important.

At its core, we desire money (or anything, really) because of the feelings we believe it will evoke. Perhaps you dream of the freedom that comes with financial security or the joy of treating your family to something special. But here's the thing, if we don't take the time to understand our emotional patterns, we might end up making choices driven by fear, scarcity, or avoidance.

Take a moment to consider some of the most common emotions tied to money:

- Fear: What if I mess things up? What if I run out? These thoughts can paralyze you, trapping you in a cycle of over-saving and avoiding healthy financial risks.
- Scarcity: These feelings whisper, "There's never enough." No matter how much you earn or save, you may find yourself constantly stressed and unsatisfied.
- Feeling Out of Control: When the numbers appear to move faster than you can keep up with, it's easy to feel helpless, which often leads to avoidance rather than action.
- Lack: This refers to the belief that money can define your worth. If "more" seems like the solution to everything, you're likely pursuing an emotional void, rather than merely financial goals.

If any of this resonates, remember, you are not alone, and you are not trapped in these feelings forever. The real power lies in recognizing them when they appear. Once you do, you can use emotions as fuel rather than as roadblocks.

For example, fear can transform into focus when you recognize it's guiding you to prepare for the future. Scarcity can foster gratitude for what you *do* have. Feeling out of control might motivate you to become more organized with your finances.

The key is to pause, take a breath, and ask yourself, "What's truly driving this decision? Is it bringing me closer to the life I desire?" By confronting these emotions directly, you can shift from reacting to *creating*, building a life where your financial choices are guided by confidence and purpose, not bound by fear.

ACTIONS & EMOTIONAL REGULATION

We all know that emotions play a significant role in our decisions, but when it comes to money, those emotions can sometimes lead us down the wrong path. Negative emotions, such as fear or shame, can drive us toward actions, or inactions, that hinder our financial success. Consider this: when you're fearful, it's easy to delay setting a plan or confronting overdue bills. You might avoid checking your bank balance when shame arises. These actions aren't about money but about attempting to escape uncomfortable feelings.

The truth is that avoiding or distracting ourselves from our emotions often creates even bigger problems. Perhaps you find yourself stress-shopping to feel better after a rough day or pushing yourself too hard to quiet that inner voice saying you're not doing enough. These quick fixes don't solve the real issue, they push those feelings down, only for them to pop up again later, stronger than before.

Here's the game-changer I discovered: processing emotions, rather than running from them, was key to transforming my relationship with money. I had to learn that it was okay to feel fear when I was starting something new, like building up savings or investing in myself. I had to sit with feelings of scarcity and remind myself that I could create abundance. Shame? It no longer had the power to keep me stuck. I started looking at my mistakes as lessons, not proof of failure.

This all ties into a practice I refer to as self-coaching. To change my financial mindset, I first had to learn how to truly *feel* my emotions. It may sound simple, but it wasn't easy. Whenever fear or shame bubbled to the surface, my instinct was always to distract myself or avoid facing it. Instead, I began naming those emotions and asking questions like, "What is this feeling really trying to tell me? What can I learn from this?" It wasn't just about calming my nerves; it was also about directing those emotions toward constructive actions.

For example, when I felt scarcity creeping in, I used it as a signal to review my budget and plan out actionable next steps. When fear came knocking, I reminded myself of my long-term goals and took just one step forward, even if it was small. And you know what? Over time, those emotions lost their grip on me. I stopped reacting impulsively and started making intentional, confident choices with my money.

The ability to regulate your emotions doesn't develop overnight, but it's one of the most powerful tools you can cultivate. By leaning into those feelings rather than avoiding them, you'll transform not only your financial mindset but also what's possible for your entire life. Every emotion you experience is an opportunity for growth. Once you recognize that, there's nothing you can't achieve.

Exercise: The Money Mindset Boardroom:
Upgrade Your Wealth Identity

Imagine stepping into an exclusive boardroom on the top floor of a high-rise. This is not just any boardroom, it belongs to the most financially successful version of you. Your Future Wealthy Self is already living the financial freedom, security, and confidence you desire. They know exactly how to handle money, investments, and success.

You take a seat at the long conference table. Across from you, your Future Wealthy Self slides a confidential folder toward you. Inside are the rules they live by, the mindset shifts that transformed their financial life.

You open the folder and see two columns. One represents the old identity, the financial beliefs that have held you back. The other reflects the wealth identity, the mindset that leads to financial control, growth, and freedom.

OLD IDENTITY VS. WEALTH IDENTITY

Old Identity (Scarcity CEO)	Wealth Identity (Powerful CEO)
"I hope I have enough money."	*"I create financial abundance."*
"I feel guilty about wealth."	*"Money allows me to create impact."*
"I don't know if I'm making the right moves."	*"I trust myself to make smart financial decisions."*
"If I don't work harder, I won't succeed."	*"My money and investments work for me."*
"Wealth is for other people."	*"Wealth is a skill, and I am mastering it."*

SIGN YOUR WEALTH LEADERSHIP AGREEMENT

Your Future Wealthy Self slides one more document toward you. It's an official agreement that states:

- I commit to thinking like a wealth builder, not a scarcity spender.
- I will make decisions based on strategy, not fear.
- I trust myself to manage and grow my money with intention.
- I operate like a CEO in my financial life.

Sign your name below.
Signature: _____
The act of signing signals a commitment to change.

STEP INTO YOUR WEALTH IDENTITY

As you rise from the table and shake hands with your Future Wealthy Self, they leave you with one final question:

"If you were already a wealth leader today, how would you handle your money differently?"

Take a deep breath. This is no longer a future version of you. You are now operating at a higher financial level.

Exit the boardroom. Step into your next level of wealth.

Take the Next Step

You've begun to uncover how emotions influence your financial decisions, now it's time to dive deeper and master your money mindset. With the Law Mother App, you'll gain powerful tools, expert guidance, and personalized resources to explore your emotions, enhance your confidence, and make intentional, impactful choices with your money.

Transform your relationship with money and build the life you deserve. Download the Law Mother App today and start your journey toward financial freedom!

To get FREE access to the Law Mother app, visit
WealthyEver.com/book or scan the QR code below to get started.

2

GROW CONTROL – ORGANIZING YOUR FINANCES FOR WEALTH AND PEACE OF MIND

GROW PERSONALLY

GROW CONTROL

GROW INCOME

When my husband and I got engaged, we were thrilled to start our lives together. We had two dreams within our reach, buying our first home and planning the perfect wedding. However, as we began to tackle the logistics, the reality of our finances hit hard. We appeared financially solid on paper, I was a six-figure litigator, and he had a steady job as a federal security contractor. Yet, when we looked closer, our financial situation was anything but organized. Without a plan, achieving both goals felt overwhelming.

It became clear that our biggest barrier was a lack of financial clarity. We sat down to evaluate our starting point, which was our current financial picture, what we desired, namely our wedding and home goals, and how we planned to achieve those through a step-by-step strategy. This sense of direction instilled confidence in us, and for the first time, managing money felt intentional rather than chaotic.

In my work as an estate planning lawyer, I noticed a pattern. During major life milestones like planning a wedding, buying a home, or having a child, people start to track their money. However, once that milestone or goal is complete, they stop tracking. Traditional financial tracking systems can feel overwhelming or limiting, which is why so many give up. Sustainable long term financial organization requires automation.

Over the years, I've worked with hundreds of families, from those living paycheck to paycheck to multimillionaires managing vast wealth. One lesson has remained clear, regardless of income level: *more money doesn't guarantee financial peace*. It's not about how much money you make but how well you organize and control it. Automated financial organization is the key to freedom, freedom that reduces stress and allows you to focus on what matters.

I've seen this truth play out time and time again. I once worked with a middle school teacher who earned a modest salary yet managed her finances precisely. She monitored her spending, clearly planned for nearly every dollar, and consistently allocated small amounts toward her goals. Despite her limited income, she felt secure and stress-free, knowing where she stood financially.

On the other hand, I counseled a highly successful plastic surgeon with a seven-figure income. Despite his earnings, he lived paycheck to paycheck, constantly stressed and overwhelmed. His high income couldn't buy him peace of mind. He lacked control, he lacked a system to manage his finances. These two examples illustrate that financial freedom comes not from how much you earn, but from the control and clarity you have over your money.

This same principal ties back to the message in Chapter 1. **Money is a relationship**. If you ignore it, it will spiral out of control. When you track and nurture it, your wealth will grow.

Before we delve into automation, this chapter focuses on achieving that initial clarity and control. Together, we will establish the foundation for true financial peace of mind.

The Framework: Bridging the Gap

Building wealth and achieving financial peace isn't about luck or guesswork but clarity. Financial clarity forms the foundation of any successful wealth-building plan. Without it, you're trying to reach a destination without knowing your starting point, where you're headed, or which path to take. This framework breaks everything down into three core stages, offering you a clear, actionable plan to move forward.

Today – Your Starting Point

The first step is understanding your current reality. Where do you stand financially? Take a full inventory of your income, expenses, assets, and liabilities. Consider this your financial "snapshot." Without clarity about your current situation, it's difficult to determine where you need to go. If this step triggers you emotionally, utilize the tools in Chapter 1.

Future – Your Financial Goals and Vision

Financial clarity also means understanding what you are working toward. What does a successful financial future look like for you? Perhaps it involves owning your dream home, sending your children to college without debt, retiring early, or engaging in pursuits that bring you joy. Defining your goals establishes a clear destination and helps keep you focused along the way.

Bridging the Gap – Actionable Steps

This is where the magic happens. Bridging the gap involves creating a step-by-step plan to transition from your current situation (Today) to your future vision (Future). These actions close the distance, whether it's paying off debt, investing strategically, or automating your savings. The key is to ensure that these steps are achievable and aligned with your long-term vision. You want to limit these steps to only those that are necessary and collectively sufficient to achieve your goals.

By understanding these three stages, you gain clarity and confidence in managing your finances. You're no longer guessing or drifting; you're following a roadmap designed to guide you toward your envisioned life.

Define Your Future: The 5 Pillars of True Wealth

Before creating a financial plan that works, we must begin by defining your future. Where do you want your life to lead? This is your opportunity to envision that life and link it to your choices today.

True wealth encompasses more than just dollars and cents. It's not solely about how much money you have in the bank, but rather about how whole and fulfilled your life feels. Concentrating on all aspects of wealth is crucial for developing a financial plan that aligns with your personal values and long-term vision. This is where the 5 Pillars of True Wealth come, a holistic framework designed to guide your financial success and overall well-being.

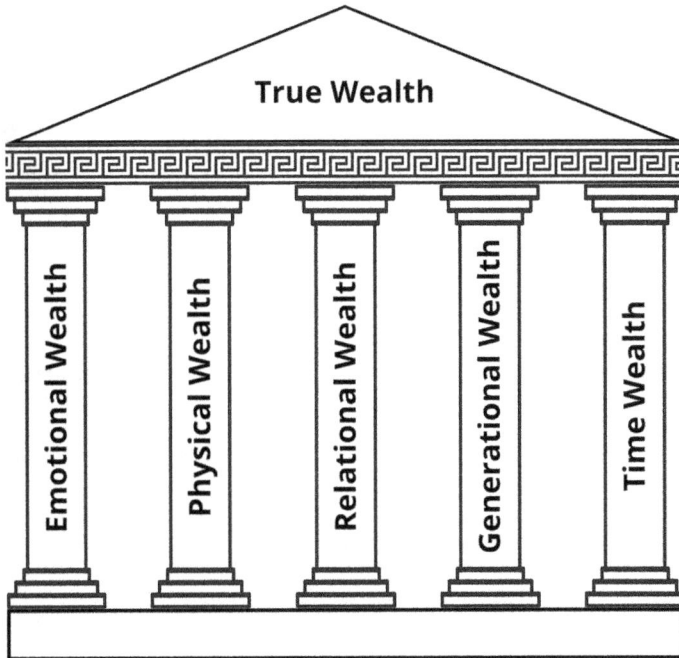

1. Emotional Wealth

This pillar represents the foundation of fulfillment. Emotional wealth involves cultivating mental peace, discovering joy in everyday life, and building resilience through life's challenges. Achieving this often means aligning your spending and goals with what brings you happiness instead of societal expectations.

Reflective Question: *In 10 years, where do you want to be with Emotional Wealth?*

Picture a life where your stress is minimal, and joy is abundant.

2. Physical Wealth = Health

Without good health, enjoying the benefits of financial success is diffi-cult. Physical well-being emphasizes your fitness and vitality, ensuring you have the energy and longevity to pursue your goals. Financially, this might involve investing in a gym membership, nutritious food, or preventive healthcare to protect your quality of life.

Reflective Question: *In 10 years, where do you want to be with Physical Wealth?*

Imagine your healthiest and most vibrant self. What does your daily routine look like?

3. Relational Wealth

Strong, meaningful connections with others are integral to true wealth. This pillar emphasizes how you nurture relationships with family, friends, and your community. Financial goals associated with this include spending quality time with loved ones, hosting gatherings, or funding experiences that unite people.

Reflective Question: *In 10 years, where do you want to be with Relational Wealth?*

Who do you see by your side, and how have you built those connections?

4. Generational Wealth

Generational wealth begins with the financial foundation you establish today. By achieving stability and growing your assets, you create a solid base for your own security and set the stage for a legacy. However, gen-erational wealth isn't just about passing down money; it's about nurtur-ing values, creating opportunities, and making a meaningful impact. This may involve teaching your children sound financial habits, start-ing a family foundation, or contributing to your community through philanthropy. Every decision you make today, whether saving, invest-ing, or giving, is a building block for the legacy you'll leave tomorrow, ensuring your influence benefits your family and the lives you touch for generations.

Reflective Question: *In 10 years, where do you want to be with Generational Wealth?*

What do you want your legacy to look like? Consider the wealth you want and the lessons, values, or financial resources you want to pass on to the next generation.

5. Time Wealth

Time is our most limited resource, and time wealth refers to the freedom to spend it in ways that matter most to you. This might include taking extended vacations, pursuing hobbies, dedicating time to causes you care about, or savoring a leisurely morning with a loved one.

Reflective Question: *In 10 years, where do you want to be with Time Wealth?*

Envision a life where you are in complete control of each day. How would you allocate your time daily?

Exercise: Your Future Self's Letter

To connect with your long-term vision of these five pillars, envision yourself 10, 20, or even 30 years in the future. Write a letter from that future version of yourself to your present self.

Describe in vivid detail how you have attained emotional, physical, relational, generational, and time wealth. Use the answers to the reflective questions to guide your vision. What does your daily life look like? Who has benefited from your choices? What small, consistent steps did you take to achieve this?

This exercise will help you set clear intentions and guide your current actions. Think big, dream boldly, and remember that no achievement is too small to include.

By defining your future within this framework and reflecting on these questions, you realize that true wealth is about more than money.

It's not merely financial, it encompasses building a life that fosters joy, health, connection, and freedom in all its dimensions.

Exercise: Your Personalized Money Roadmap

This exercise ties back to the introduction where we began envisioning your future, turning that vision into a concrete plan. Your personalized money roadmap bridges the gap between dreaming and doing, guiding you through clear, actionable financial steps to bring your ideal life closer to reality. By connecting your aspirations with tangible goals, you can move forward with confidence and clarity. Here's how to break it down into three steps:

1. Price Your Dream Life

Reflect on the vision you crafted for your future and incorporate numbers into it. Begin by estimating the costs associated with key aspects of your ideal life. For instance:

- Dream home: Research the cost of your ideal type of home in the location you dream of living. Maybe it's $500,000 for a suburban house or $1.2 million for a high-rise city condo.
- Vacations: Assess the expenses required to visit your bucket-list destinations. A two-week family trip to Europe may cost around $15,000, whereas a week at a beach resort could be about $5,000.
- Philanthropy: If giving back is part of your dream, determine the amount you would like to donate each year, perhaps $10,000 to support charities or causes that matter to you.

Putting these figures down clarifies the scope of your goals, while creating real targets to aim for.

2. Look One Year Ahead

Long-term dreams are achieved one step at a time. Start by assessing the upcoming 12 months and establishing actionable goals that correspond with your larger vision. Examples include:

- Saving for a down payment: If your dream home costs $500,000 and requires a 20% down payment, aim to save $50,000 over four years by breaking it into $12,500 yearly chunks.
- Paying off credit card debt: Set a goal to reduce high-interest debt by $5,000 this year by cutting nonessential expenses and reallocating funds.
- Starting a side hustle: Contribute an additional $500 each month to your dream fund by utilizing a skill or passion, like freelancing or selling handmade products online.

Small, manageable tasks build momentum, making larger goals feel less daunting and much more achievable.

3. Calculate Your Ballpark Retirement Number

While immediate objectives are essential, long-term planning is valuable to your overall strategy. Work through this straightforward calculation:

- Step 1: Identify your desired annual retirement lifestyle cost. For example, you might want $60,000 annually to cover housing, travel, hobbies, and everyday living expenses.
- Step 2: Multiply that number by 25 to find your retirement savings target. For $60,000 annually, you'd aim for $1.5 million in total savings ($60,000 x 25).
- Step 3: Break it down, for example, saving $10,000 yearly for 30 years (plus compound interest) might put you well within reach of your goal.

This calculation shows that financial independence may be closer than it seems. Even modest, consistent savings today can build a secure and abundant tomorrow.

Why This is a Ballpark Number

It's important to understand that this calculation provides a broad estimate intended for visioning purposes. Your actual retirement savings
goal may fluctuate based on factors such as inflation, healthcare costs,
unexpected expenses, and the investment returns you achieve.

Furthermore, everyone's retirement needs vary. Your desired lifestyle may evolve over time, or you might have specific plans, such as
relocating to a more affordable area or traveling extensively. For this
reason, it's important to regularly review and adjust this figure as you
advance in your financial planning.

Personal Reflection

Revisiting the roadmap introduced in the beginning, you now see how
connecting dreams to numbers transforms them into actionable steps.
Small actions, like automating monthly contributions or eliminating
unnecessary expenses, create a ripple effect that gets you closer to
your goals.

Your roadmap isn't just a plan; it's a guide to living purposefully.
Whether it's budgeting for a dream vacation, hitting debt milestones, or
investing for retirement, every step forward is a win. By combining your
vision with deliberate choices, you're designing a life that's fulfilling in
the present and secure in the future.

Exercise: Create Your Wealth Vision One-Sheet

Your financial vision deserves to be both inspiring and actionable.
By condensing it into a simple, one-page document or graphic, you
create a powerful tool to keep your goals tangible, motivational, and
always within reach. This Wealth Vision One-Sheet acts as your personal guide, helping align various aspects of your life with your ultimate
goals. Here's how to create one:

1. Your 5 Wealth Goals

Focus on the 5 holistic wealth pillars—Physical, Emotional, Financial, Social, and Spiritual wealth, and create specific, actionable goals for each to build balance and fulfillment.

2. A Clear 1-Year Goal

Highlight a practical, achievable objective for the next 12 months that ties each pillar together.

3. A Significant 10-Year Goal

Create an ambitious long-term target to guide your focus and ensure sustainable progress.

4. Your 20 Year or Retirement Goal

Clarify your vision of a 20 year or ideal retirement supported by the wealth you've built across all life pillars.

Example Wealth Vision One-Sheet

Category	12 Months	5 Years	20 Years
Emotional Wealth	Write in a gratitude journal 5 days a week focusing on 3 positive moments daily.	Complete 60 guided therapy or personal development sessions to enhance self-awareness.	Become a mentor in emotional well-being, sharing strategies through workshops or writing a book.

Category	12 Months	5 Years	20 Years
Physical Wealth	Exercise 4 times a week for 30 minutes and maintain a balanced diet tracked weekly.	Run a marathon and achieve a physical wellness benchmark like a healthy BMI or fitness milestone.	Be a symbol of vitality, participating in adventurous activities like climbing a mountain or biking across a region.
Relational Wealth	Have intentional, meaningful conversations with 1 loved one weekly.	Organize and host 5 family or friends' reunions to strengthen bonds and build traditions.	Create a legacy of relationships, such as establishing annual family councils or writing a family history.
Generational Wealth	Save $6,000 and open an investment account for future family needs or education.	Own and grow a diversified portfolio valued at $250,000 earmarked for generational assets.	Leave a lasting financial legacy by creating a $2M family endowment supporting education or community causes.

Category	12 Months	5 Years	20 Years
Time Wealth	Dedicate 2 hours weekly to a passion project or personal growth activity.	Reduce low-value time commitments by 25%, freeing up at least 5 extra hours per week.	Achieve ultimate freedom by retiring early and dedicating 50% of your time to passion-driven work and meaningful experiences.

Using Your One-Sheet Effectively

Put this one-sheet in a visible and strategic location, such as your home office or digital planner. Regularly review it, updating goals as you accomplish milestones or adjust priorities. Balancing these five wealth pillars creates a harmonious and purposeful life that aligns with your most important values.

This approach keeps your vision grounded in holistic growth, enabling you to excel in every facet of wealth.

Exercise: Create Your Wealth Map (Starting Today)

Before crafting your financial future, it's essential to understand your current situation. By mapping out your financial picture, you clarify your starting point and identify the steps needed to bridge the gap to your goals. This process organizes your financial life and offers a motivating snapshot of your progress over time. Here's how to create your wealth map:

Step 1. List Your Assets

Begin by listing all your valuable possessions. This encompasses both tangible and intangible assets. Organize them into categories for a thorough overview:

- Real Estate: Include your primary home, rental properties, or land holdings.
- Bank Accounts: List checking, savings, and any international accounts.
- Investments: Document stocks, bonds, mutual funds, ETFs, or retirement accounts like a 401(k) or IRA.
- Life Insurance: Consider policies with cash surrender values.
- Businesses: Own a side hustle or enterprise? Include its estimated value.
- Alternative Investments: Factor in items like cryptocurrency, collectibles, or art.
- Personal Property: Include vehicles, jewelry, or other high-value items.

Add up the total value of these to calculate your *Total Assets.*

Step 2. Identify Your Liabilities

Next, document everything you owe. Liabilities represent your current financial obligations. Categorize them as follows:

- Debts: Record credit card balances and personal loans.
- Mortgages: Include outstanding balances on real estate loans.
- Student Loans: Total up outstanding education-related debt.
- Car Loans: Add any remaining vehicle payments.
- Other Financial Obligations: Examples include medical debt or tax liabilities.

Add these numbers to determine your *Total Liabilities.*

Step 3. Calculate Your Net Worth

Net worth is the essential figure that indicates how much you own after considering your expenses. debts. Here's how to calculate it:

Total Net Worth Formula

[Total Net Worth = Total Assets - Total Liabilities]
For example, if your assets total $500,000 and your liabilities are $200,000, your net worth is $300,000.

Investable Net Worth

This figure excludes assets that cannot be quickly converted into cash, such as your primary residence or personal property. To calculate your *Investable Net Worth*, subtract these non-liquid assets from your Total Net Worth.

Step 4. Use Simple Tools to Stay on Track

Tools such as *Wealthy Ever After* can help you easily visualize these numbers. Enter your data to break down your net worth and monitor progress toward your goals. Consider updating this information quarterly or annually to reflect changes such as income growth, debt reduction, or investment gains.

Why Understanding Your Starting Point Matters

Understanding your current financial position is not just helpful, it is essential. Your net worth is a benchmark, enabling you to see how far you must go to achieve your goals. It provides perspective, emphasizes areas for improvement, and guides you on what actions are needed next.

By creating your wealth map, you are laying the foundation for a stronger financial future. It's your guide to navigating the path from where you are today to where you dream of being tomorrow.

Bridging the Gap: Your Stairway to Wealthy

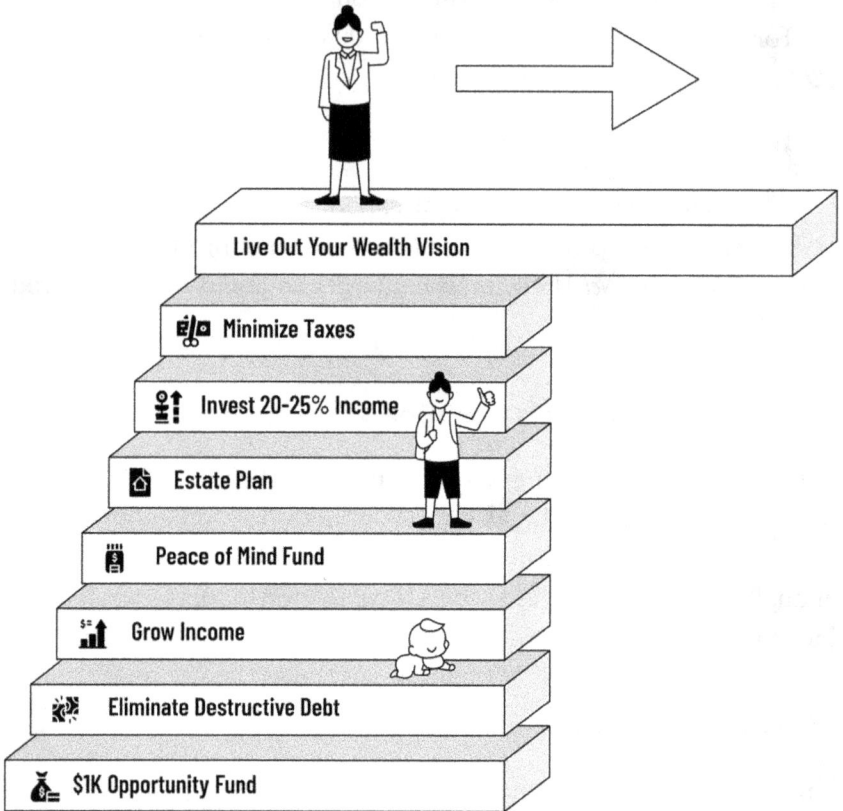

Live Out Your Wealth Vision

Minimize Taxes

Invest 20-25% Income

Estate Plan

Peace of Mind Fund

Grow Income

Eliminate Destructive Debt

$1K Opportunity Fund

Achieving your financial vision requires a systematic approach. The Stairway to Wealthy outlines the essential steps to financial stability and long-term prosperity. Each stage builds upon the previous one, creating a pathway toward sustainable financial success.

Stage 1. Opportunity Fund

Many people refer to this initial savings as an "emergency fund," aimed at preparing for unexpected issues such as car repairs or surprise medical bills. While this is accurate, the term "emergency fund" can provoke a negative emotional response by fostering a mindset of fear and scarcity.

Instead, we call it an *opportunity fund* because it changes your approach to financial preparedness. When you see this money as a resource for opportunities instead of just for emergencies, it transforms your mindset toward empowerment and proactive planning. This subtle shift in language enables you to view your financial buffer as a tool for stability and growth.

Why This Shift in Terminology Matters

Words influence how we think and feel about situations. Referring to it as an opportunity fund encourages you to envision how this money can relieve stress while giving you the flexibility to tackle life's surprises confidently. It's not merely about addressing emergencies; it's about having the freedom to say "yes" to unexpected opportunities or solving issues without resorting to debt.

Examples of How an Opportunity Fund Works:

- Car Repairs Turned into Reliable Transport
  Imagine your car breaks down. Instead of reacting with panic, you calmly tap into your opportunity fund to fix it. The result? You stay on the road, maintain your income opportunities, and keep your stress level low.
- Health Costs Managed with Ease
  If an unexpected medical bill arises, your opportunity fund is prepared. Rather than worrying about how to cover it, you address the issue without adding financial strain.
- The Power to Say Yes
  Perhaps an unexpected opportunity arises, such as a deeply discounted flight ticket to visit family or a professional course you've been eager to take. Your opportunity fund offers the financial flexibility to seize these moments without hesitation.

By starting with a manageable goal such as saving $1,000, you establish a foundation of security and confidence. This small opportunity fund prepares you for the unexpected while keeping you focused on possibilities rather than fear. It's protection with a positive purpose.

Action Steps

- Save $1,000 quickly by cutting unnecessary expenses or selling unneeded items.
- Keep this fund in a separate, easily accessible high yield savings account. Keeping your opportunity fund in a high-yield savings account is smart because it offers better interest rates to grow your savings over time while ensuring easy access to your money when you need it most.

Stage 2. Eliminate Destructive Debt

High-interest debt, such as credit cards or payday loans, can hinder your ability to build wealth. Focus on rapidly paying off these debts to improve your cash flow and alleviate financial strain and stress.

Action Steps

- Compile all debts and prioritize them by interest rate or balance. Pay them off using strategies such as the Debt Snowball (starting with the smallest debts) or the Debt Avalanche (paying off the highest interest first).
- Avoid taking on additional debt while completing this stage.

Stage 3. Grow Your Income

At this stage, the focus shifts to actively growing your income, a pivotal step toward achieving greater financial stability, resilience, and independence. Expanding your earning potential helps cover your current needs and positions you to seize future opportunities and pursue long-term financial goals. By diversifying your income across five key income streams, you can establish a well-rounded foundation for growth. You will learn more about this in Chapter 3.

Stage 4. Build Your Peace of Mind Fund

Imagine a life where unexpected challenges no longer throw you off course, where financial security becomes the foundation for your dreams. Once you've tackled high-interest debt, it's time to take a big step toward lasting stability by creating your Peace of Mind Fund. This is more than just a financial buffer; it's your safeguard against life's bigger surprises, like job loss or unforeseen emergencies, and it's the key to sleeping soundly at night, knowing you're prepared for anything.

A Peace of Mind Fund covering 3–6 months of essential expenses shields you from major financial disruptions, giving you breathing room to focus on solutions rather than scrambling for quick fixes. It's not just about surviving tough times; it's about thriving through them with confidence and control.

Action Steps to Build Your Fund

- Calculate Your Goal

  Start by figuring out what 3–6 months of necessary expenses look like for you. Consider key needs like rent or mortgage payments, utilities, groceries, insurance, and transportation. This number is your personalized safety net, ready to catch you when the unexpected happens.

- Save Steadily with Automation

  Achieving your goal doesn't require overhauling everything at once; it's a gradual, empowering process. Establish an automated savings plan to consistently direct a portion of your income toward this fund. Whether it takes months or years, every step forward is a step toward freedom.

- Choose Growth and Flexibility

  Protect your Peace of Mind Fund by keeping it in a high-yield savings account, where it can grow with higher interest rates while remaining easily accessible when you need it. This combination of growth and liquidity ensures that your safety net works for you without sacrificing availability.

Why This Fund Transforms Your Journey

Your Peace of Mind Fund isn't just about money in the bank; it's about the freedom to face adversity with grace, the courage to take calculated risks, and the confidence that you're building a financial life grounded in security. With this fund in place, you'll be empowered to handle life's ups and downs, knowing you've already taken steps to secure your future.

Celebrate this stage as a significant milestone in your wealth-building journey, marking a transition from responding with worry to engaging with strength. Your Peace of Mind Fund is not just a safety net; it serves as a foundation for greater dreams and opportunities ahead. Continue moving forward, step by step, toward the abundance and stability you deserve.

Stage 5. Set up or Update Your Estate Plan

An estate plan ensures that your wealth is distributed according to your wishes while protecting your family from legal complications. This planning for the future brings peace of mind as you secure your financial legacy. If you're unsure where to begin, don't worry. Chapter 6 will provide a deeper dive into estate planning, covering its key components, actionable steps, and practical tips for creating a plan tailored to your unique needs.

Stage 6. Invest 20–25% of Income

Consistently investing a portion of your income is essential for long-term wealth building. By allocating 20 to 25% of your gross income to investment opportunities, you allow your money to grow over time and work for your future.

Action Steps:

- Maximize contributions to retirement accounts like 401(k)s or IRAs.
- Diversify your investments with low-cost index funds, stocks, and bonds.
- Reference Chapters 4 and 5 for detailed investment strategies.

Stage 7. Minimize Taxes

To keep more of what you earn, it's crucial to leverage strategies that reduce your tax burden. Maximize contributions to tax-advantaged accounts like 401(k)s, IRAs, and HSAs while considering alternative investments such as real estate or municipal bonds to diversify and lower taxable income. Business owners can take advantage of deductions for operating expenses, home offices, and retirement plans tailored for entrepreneurs. Combining these strategies with professional advice ensures that you effectively utilize available credits and deductions. For more insights into alternative approaches and business-specific tax strategies, explore Chapter 8.

Stage 8. Live Out Your Wealth Vision

The ultimate stage of the Stairway to Wealthy involves reaching a point where your resources align seamlessly with your passions, values, and dreams across all areas of life. Here, fulfillment replaces financial limitations, enabling you to fully realize your wealth vision. By integrating the principles of growth, multiplication, and acceleration with the five wealth pillars, you can cultivate a balanced, purpose-driven life that evolves alongside your five, ten-year, and retirement goals.

Living your wealth vision involves maintaining financial health and continually evaluating and expanding your wealth to foster a life filled with purpose, joy, and lasting impact.

For deeper insights and practical strategies to sustain and enhance your wealth vision, refer to Chapter 9, which discusses continuously growing and adapting your wealth blueprint to maximize its impact on your life and legacy.

Building Momentum at Every Stage

Every stage of the Stairway to Wealthy builds on the previous one, solidifying your financial future step-by-step. For example, having a fully funded Peace of Mind Fund prevents emergencies from derailing your progress, while eliminating destructive debt paves the way for consistent investing.

Automating Your Stairway to Wealthy

To stay on track, consider setting up automatic transfers for your savings, debt repayment, and investment accounts. Automation reduces decision fatigue and seamlessly builds momentums.

By aligning your actions with the structure of the Stairway to Wealthy you'll confidently move from financial uncertainty to stability and prosperity. This systematic approach transforms your financial reality into the life of abundance you've envisioned. From achieving small milestones like an Opportunity Fund to living out your wealth vision, you're creating a legacy of lasting success.

CLOSING: TAKE CONTROL, GROW CONTROL

When I first committed to taking control of my finances, I had no idea how far it would lead me. One of my earliest and perhaps most meaningful milestones was purchasing our dream home, a cozy, light-filled space in a neighborhood I had always admired. It wasn't an impulsive decision; it stemmed from a place of confidence, built on a foundation of organizing my finances, setting clear goals, and working toward them in a focused manner. That same clarity also enabled me to plan and host a $10K mountain wedding for 60 of our closest friends and family. It was simple yet magical, filled with laughter, love, and connections. Being able to enjoy that special day without financial anxiety made it even more extraordinary. (Curious about how we pulled it off? Check out the appendix for our wedding budgeting tips!)

Once I realized the possibilities of financial clarity and control, I applied those principles to various aspects of my life. One of my proudest achievements was growing my law firm from $0 to seven figures. What began as a small dream evolved into a thriving business, thanks to my focus on discipline, structure, and prioritizing my resources. I reinvested wisely, automated operations wherever possible, and remained committed to long-term sustainability, even when instant gratification tempted me. This success reinforced for me that financial clarity isn't just about money; it's about creating freedom and the ability to act confidently on your dreams.

Your Path to Peace of Mind

These milestones did not rely on luck or overly complicated strategies; they originated from organizing my finances, prioritizing tasks, and taking consistent action. The peace and confidence I gained from managing my money enabled me to transform abstract goals into achievable realities.

You can achieve the same transformation. With tools like the Law Mother app and the steps outlined in this book, you are equipped to take control of your financial story. Begin today by following these simple steps:

- Define Your Future—Clarify what financial freedom means for you.
- Map Your Reality—Understand your current financial position by listing your assets and liabilities and calculating a snapshot of your net worth.
- Start Your Financial Transformation by Following the Stairway to Wealthy to tackle your goals in a structured and confident way.

The choices you make today will determine your future success. Taking control of your finances is the first step to creating the life you've been dreaming of.

To get **FREE** access to the Law Mother app visit WealthyEver.com/book or scan the **QR** code below and get started.

3

GROW YOUR INCOME – GROW YOUR EARNING POWER WITH MULTIPLE INCOME STREAMS

BREAKING FREE FROM THE TRADITIONAL PATH

I began my legal career pursuing the traditional notion of success, long hours, late nights, and weekend work. That's the narrative in the legal field, isn't it? You're praised for pulling all-nighters and rewarded for sacrificing your personal time. At first, I believed this was just how it had to be, but deep down, it didn't align with my true desires.

I envisioned starting a family one day and didn't want my life to be defined by missing those moments because I was too preoccupied with billing hours.

And so, I found myself driving ever forward, toward what? One day, it hit me, I wasn't driving toward success; I was heading into a trap. My income was tied to my hours, and there was no way around that hard ceiling. No matter how hard I pushed, there were only so many hours a day. I was stuck trading time for money. But I wanted more, not just more income, but more life. I desired time, freedom, and purpose. That realization became the wake-up call that set me on an unexpected path, one where I would learn about passion, income streams, and creating a meaningful life.

Before we continue, I want to clarify that this chapter isn't solely about starting a business. It doesn't matter if you love what you're doing and have no intention of leaving your salaried job. I'm offering tools and strategies to give you options and effectively diversify your income in a way that aligns with your goals without disrupting the career you already find fulfilling.

LESSONS IN EFFORT, ALIGNMENT, AND GROWTH

Breaking free from my cycle of trading time for money was anything but smooth. I dove into side hustles with the fervor of someone desperate for change. I created an online course on building websites, started a blog, and even experimented with software products. The results? Only frustration. Every endeavor drained my time, resources, and energy. Why? Because none of them aligned with who I was or what I believed in, and on some level, I recognized it. I kept spinning my wheels, expending tremendous effort while getting nowhere.

It wasn't until much later that I recognized my larger mistake. I had bought into the myth of easy income, the belief that passive income was a set-and-forget concept, allowing money to roll in effortlessly. It sounded too good to be true, and it was. The reality? Passive income isn't genuinely passive. It requires intention, alignment, and effort.

A mentor's story illustrates this point. He once launched what he believed was his dream business, selling educational CDs. The plan seemed solid initially; for a moment, it looked like the CDs were selling themselves. However, reality quickly set in. He spent countless hours stuffing envelopes and managing everything from logistics to customer service. Worse yet, he wasn't passionate about the product, which showed. Instead of providing him with freedom, what he envisioned turned into another grind, tethered to work he didn't enjoy.

But here's the important lesson: there's a spectrum regarding passive income. There is no such thing as truly "effortless" income; however, certain investments and activities can be relatively passive and still rewarding. Over time, dividend-paying stocks, rental properties with reliable management, or scalable online ventures can become less hands-on if built intentionally. The critical factor is ensuring that your chosen path aligns with your long-term values, skills, and goals.

CREATING MEANINGFUL OPPORTUNITIES

For me, that was a life-changing pivot. I decided to focus on opportunities that felt authentic and meaningful. I had just undergone a personal transformation at that time, losing 40 pounds and winning a fitness competition. I shared my progress online, and soon, women began reaching out, seeking help with their health journeys. Inspired by their interest, I delved deeper into studying nutrition and weightlifting, eventually creating a fitness group for women. For the first time, I wasn't merely chasing income but building something aligned with my purpose.

I worked on the fitness group during nights and weekends, and, by day, I worked as a lawyer. I poured my heart into the fitness program, and it showed. Women didn't just stay for the results, they remained for the community I had built and the effort I dedicated to it. This venture provided me with two invaluable gifts. The first was supplemental income, but the second, and far more important, was the confidence that I could create something real, impactful, and aligned with my values.

Buoyed by that confidence, I took another leap and launched my own law firm. Starting a business brought unexpected challenges, but it was incredibly rewarding. For the first time, I could shape my career and life according to my rules, not someone else's. I diversified my income streams and began designing a life that reflected my goals and values.

THE POWER OF DIVERSIFICATION

This journey taught me a fundamental truth about wealth. It's not just about making money or leaving a full-time job to start a business. True wealth lies in diversification. Relying solely on one income stream, a salaried job or a single entrepreneurial venture, makes you vulnerable. By diversifying your income, you create stability, freedom, and, most importantly, the ability to live on your own terms.

And here's what I want you to know: you don't need to leave your job to make this work. If you're thriving in your current career, you can add financial layers that support your goals without disrupting what brings you joy. True freedom isn't about walking away from something you love; it's about ensuring all aspects of your life are aligned, diverse, and purposeful. That's how you carve out a life that works for you and how everything begins to change.

WHAT'S NEXT

Here's what you can look forward to in this chapter:

- For Those Growing Their Income: We will explore ways to enhance your earnings, including strategies for negotiating raises, acquiring new skills, and diversifying your income streams. You'll gain practical tools to establish a solid foundation from active to portfolio-based income.
- For High Earners Aiming to Optimize: If you're already earning well but want to secure your future, you'll learn to optimize cash flow, reduce taxes intelligently, and invest strategically to build long-term wealth.

Income diversification isn't just about money; it's about creating options and crafting a life that aligns with your values and aspirations. Whether you're just starting or are already well-established financially, this chapter will help you rethink what's possible. Each of us will follow our unique path, and the power to take control of your life rests in your hands.

Diversifying Your Income – Exploring the Five Key Income Streams

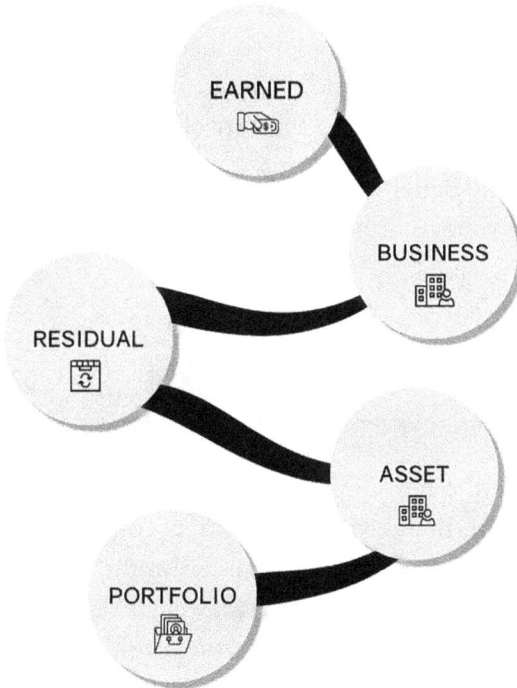

This chapter is about giving you the tools and understanding to diversify your income and build a solid financial foundation. Here, we'll detail five key income streams and strategies for integrating them into your life. These streams, the cornerstones of financial resilience, are Earned Income, Business Income, Asset-Based Income, Residual Income, and Portfolio Income.

While this chapter introduces the concepts and strategies behind each stream, don't worry if it feels like a lot to take in at once. Chapter 9 will help you prioritize your income streams, based on your unique goals and where you are now. These chapters provide the "what" and "how" for your financial transformation.

Let's explore the potential of each income stream and the opportunities they offer.

A. EARNED INCOME (ACTIVE)

Earned income, the most familiar stream, comes directly from your work, salaries, hourly wages, or freelance gig payments. It's often the primary source of income and the financial base to build upon.

Here are strategies to make the most of your active income right now:

- Negotiate Better Pay: Show your value by presenting clear examples of your contributions. Research industry standards to make a strong case for a raise.

Five Steps to Negotiate Better Pay

1) Frame for gain and keep your eye on the prize

People who see the negotiation as risky are more conservative in their asks and miss out. Before you go into the negotiation, think about what you could win. When you put your offer on the table, don't be afraid, be specific and bold. Ask for more than what feels comfortable. You can always negotiate down from your starting position, but you can rarely, if ever, negotiate up from a low starting base

2) Prepare and practice

Consider how your proposed pay increase and/or promotion could be of value to your boss and the company. Your boss will be more likely to agree that it is not just a "win" for you if they see potential benefit to them and the company.

Possible ways to frame this:

- Keeping a valuable employee
- Additional responsibilities
- Reducing risk for the company
- Credibility with stakeholders (customers, regulatory agencies…)

As you prepare, consider:

» How do I think the negotiation process will unfold?
» How might my boss react and respond when I ask what I want?
» What may be the likely objections? How will I respond to those objections?

Do some dry runs with a friend or mentor to help you rehearse. Ask them to play devil's advocate to challenge and test your arguments.

3) Pick your timing

Pick a time when your boss will be the most receptive. You don't want to approach them when they are busy or have just come out of a stressful meeting.

If you've just landed a big win at work, you've already positively got your boss' attention, and that could be a great time to make the ask.

Remember that it's not the right time to negotiate if you feel anxious or tired. Anxiety is a natural emotion during negotiations, particularly when the topic is salary, and impacts your effectiveness.

In a simulated experiment, Brooks and Schweitzer (2011) found that anxious individuals made weaker first offers, responded more quickly (and less thoughtfully) to each move their counterpart made, and were more likely to exit negotiations early. Ultimately, they secured deals that were 12% less financially advantageous. If you find your mind racing during the conversation, focus on deep breathing. Pausing to breathe will allow your heart rate to slow down, making it easier to reflect and respond calmly.

4) Approach it like a conversation

The more you try to understand your boss' situation and perspective, the more insights you'll have to make your case and reach some agreement successfully.

Research reveals that the more you can "get inside their head" and understand their perspective, the better placed you will be.

5) Make the ask

This is your opportunity, so embrace it.

When you ask, use the data you collected to support your points, whether it's the going salaries for people with your experience or details on how your proposal will improve the organization's profitability.

You aim to back up your claim. You need to explain that what you are asking for is fair, reasonable, and in the other person's interests.

Negotiating is a mixture of art and psychology. And it's not easy.

Nailing it requires practice. Take time to prepare and practice to help you stay calm and confident during the conversation. The importance of negotiating to get what you want cannot be overestimated. Now's the time to step up.

- Upskill Strategically: Gaining expertise or certifications can lead to promotions or entry into higher-paying roles. Online platforms make this accessible and affordable.

  Offer to take on some of the tasks others tend to avoid. This will benefit your organization and may help build relationships with coworkers. Ensure that your efforts are visible to your boss and their boss, perhaps using humor by joking about those unpleasant, undesirable tasks.

- Leverage Your Skills Elsewhere: Platforms such as Fiverr and Upwork enable you to discover freelance opportunities, transforming your existing skills into additional income.

Increasing your active income will enhance your capacity to support other income streams, which we will explore in more detail.

B. BUSINESS INCOME

Business income provides an opportunity to earn money through entrepreneurial ventures. This may involve starting something new or acquiring an existing business. Either path can significantly increase your income, and your approach will depend on your resources, interests, and time.

Starting Your Own Business

This can range from launching a side hustle to establishing a full-time business. Begin with small steps, sell baked goods at a local market or provide consulting services in your expertise. Platforms like Etsy or Shopify can assist you in scaling your efforts as you progress.

Purchasing an Existing Business

Purchasing an established business bypasses the groundwork phase, enabling you to access immediate revenue opportunities.

- Benefits:
  - » Generates income right away.
  - » Includes a solid customer base and established systems.
  - » Offers potential for growth, like expanding services or increasing marketing efforts.

- Considerations:
  - » Always perform due diligence by reviewing financials, liabilities, and the rationale for the sale.
  - » Explore financing options like SBA loans to make ownership more accessible.
  - » Align the type of business with your interests and long-term goals.

For example, you might buy a thriving online store and refine operations while adding your unique touch. Business income creates vast opportunities and a sense of ownership over your financial path.

C. ASSET-BASED INCOME

This stream leverages ownership of physical and creative assets to produce earnings. Though it typically requires an upfront investment of time, money, or both, the long-term gains can be substantial.

- Real Estate: Rental income is a classic example, but you can start smaller by investing in real estate crowdfunding platforms.

- Small Assets: Smaller-scale items like equipment or vehicles can generate income when rented out.

Asset-based income focuses on building value from the resources you own or create, setting a solid foundation for future wealth.

D. RESIDUAL INCOME

Residual income allows you to benefit from an initial investment of effort or money, creating ongoing cash flow.

- Digital Products: Create enduring content such as courses, templates, or eBooks that can be sold repeatedly without constant updates.
- Content Creation: Generate revenue through ad placements or subscriptions by producing engaging video or written content on platforms like YouTube or Substack.
- Affiliate Marketing: Generate sales by promoting products you are enthusiastic about, particularly if you already have an audience.

This stream supports your financial growth with reduced day-to-day involvement over time, making it a crucial long-term goal.

E. PORTFOLIO INCOME: GROWING WEALTH THROUGH INVESTMENT

Investing in financial markets provides a powerful way to build wealth over time. While this may initially feel overwhelming, it's more accessible than it appears when you adopt the right approach. By concentrating on assets like stocks, bonds, and ETFs, you can establish a solid foundation for a secure financial future. If these concepts seem new, don't worry, we'll delve into them in greater detail in Chapters 4 and 5.

When it comes to investing, key concepts like assessing risk tolerance and setting clear financial goals are essential. Your comfort level with market risks and your vision for the future will influence your selected strategies. For instance, you may be inclined towards bonds or dividend-paying stocks if your goal is to generate stable income. Conversely, if you're pursuing growth and are eager for higher returns, you might concentrate on stocks or ETFs with greater growth potential.

The tools and strategies we will cover in later chapters will help guide you as you align your investments with your unique goals and preferences. Investing does not have to be intimidating; with some knowledge and planning, it can become one of the cornerstones of your financial success.

Looking Ahead to Your Blueprint

The five income streams serve as building blocks for financial security and growth. Implementing all these strategies at once can feel overwhelming, and that's okay.

This chapter introduces possibilities and equips you with actionable ideas for each stream. When we reach Chapter 9, we'll shift our focus to help you prioritize and plan. You'll learn to assess your current situation, identify which streams align with your lifestyle and goals, and confidently take the first steps.

Consider this chapter your toolkit. Explore the ideas that resonate with you and trust that your personalized financial path will emerge as we progress through the book. Every stream has its place, and with careful planning, you'll create a financial picture that aligns with the life you envision.

If You're a High Earner – Diversify and Optimize

Reaching a high-earning stage in your financial life is not merely an accomplishment, it's an opportunity. With your income level, the focus should shift toward diversifying your wealth-building strategies and ensuring that your financial decisions are as tax-efficient as possible. At this stage, your goal is to work smarter, not harder, with the resources you've developed.

This is the ideal moment to begin considering options beyond a single income source and explore the balance and growth potential of a diversified financial strategy. Additionally, pay close attention to how tax optimization can help maintain and enhance your earnings.

Diversify Across the Five Streams

High earners like you are in a unique position to benefit from multiple income streams more quickly and effectively. Exploring diverse income avenues isn't just about protection; it's a way to amplify your earnings and create multiple engines for growth.

- Portfolio Income: Use your income to build a robust portfolio of stocks, bonds, and ETFs. With diversification, you can reduce risk and enjoy long-term compounding.
- Business Income: Consider starting or acquiring a business, as mentioned earlier in this chapter. Your resources provide opportunities like purchasing a franchise or investing in established ventures.
- Rental Income: Investing in real estate, such as rental properties or REITs, provides consistent cash flow, tax benefits, and potential for long-term appreciation.
- Active Income: Just because you are a high earner doesn't mean you overlook your primary income. Keep refining skills and seizing growth opportunities in your field or business.
- Royalty or Intellectual Property Income: If you have a unique idea, talent, or expertise, turning it into passive income streams through royalties, books, or licensing is another way to grow your wealth.

Diversifying across these streams ensures your financial future is not dependent on a single source. You create stability and leverage your income to explore multiple avenues for growth.

Prioritize Tax Efficiency

At this income level, one of the greatest opportunities lies in preserving your earnings by minimizing taxes, legally and strategically. Taxes can significantly diminish your earnings, but you can keep more of your hard-earned dollars with thoughtful planning.

- Leverage Retirement Accounts: Maximize contributions to 401(k)s, IRAs, and HSAs to save on taxes now and build future wealth.
- Explore Tax-Advantaged Investments: Investments like real estate can offer tax-free income or significant tax deductions.
- Optimize Deductions and Credits: Partner with a tax professional to uncover possible deductions, such as charitable contributions, and credits that apply specifically to high-income individuals.
- Organization Matters: Organizing your finances and actively tracking deductions when managing multiple income streams is crucial.

We'll cover specific strategies and actionable advice on tax efficiency and retirement planning in Chapter 8. This will give you the tools needed to streamline your approach and ensure you keep as much as possible from every income stream.

A Pivotal Moment for Your Financial Future

As a high earner, this isn't merely about celebrating your success, it marks a turning point. Your decisions regarding diversification and tax optimization will shape your financial future. By strategically distributing your wealth across five income streams and engaging in smart tax planning, you're not just managing your finances, you're securing a legacy of stability, freedom, and growth.

Consider diversification and tax efficiency as essential keys to achieving financial independence. With careful planning, you can preserve your cherished lifestyle while ensuring your wealth continues to grow and serve you for many years ahead.

TAKING CHARGE OF YOUR FUTURE: DIVERSIFY INCOME, AND EMPOWER FINANCIAL GROWTH

I still reflect on those early, unsuccessful side hustles. I was looking for a quick fix, one path to financial freedom that didn't exist then. Each failure taught me something important. I learned that your relationship with money is as dynamic as your life, it changes based on your values, priorities, and goals. I discovered that diversifying how you earn money is the best way to achieve financial security. And most importantly, I realized that there's immense power in taking ownership of your earning potential.

Those failures weren't failures after all; they were stepping stones. They guided me toward building my successful law firm and, ultimately, a life where I'm in control, not just of my income, but of my future.

You have the power to take control of your financial destiny. It won't happen overnight. Start by building meaningful income streams that align with your goals and watch how this confidence ripples through every other area of your financial life.

LOOKING AHEAD

By exploring this chapter's five key income streams and understanding the importance of mastering credit, you've taken vital steps toward creating a safer, more adaptable financial future. Diversification offers stability, not only through steady income but also through the confidence that comes from knowing you're not reliant on a single source. Whether you're just beginning your financial journey or a high earner ready to optimize, the strategies outlined here, along with a foundation of strong credit, serve as your roadmap to long-term success.

ACTION ITEMS

To set yourself up for success, start with these steps today:

1. Identify Income Opportunities: Evaluate your skills, interests, and available resources to discover potential additional income streams. For example, consider whether investing in ETFs, pursuing a rental property, or transforming a creative hobby into income aligns with your goals.
2. Set Clear Financial Goals: Define what financial freedom means to you. Whether it's saving for a home, starting a business, or achieving work-life balance, having well-defined goals will guide your decisions.

3. Begin Small: You don't have to revamp everything all at once. Start by investing small amounts in index funds, dedicating time to a single side project, or exploring a new business idea. Gradual progress accumulates quickly.

4. Track Finances: Understanding where your money goes is the first step toward using it wisely.

5. Invest in Learning: Keep expanding your knowledge of diversification, financial tools, and credit management. Educate yourself to make decisions that align with your overall financial plan confidently.

Achieving financial success is a series of small, deliberate steps. Diversify your income and empower yourself with the tools and knowledge to secure a brighter financial future.

To get FREE access to the Law Mother app visit WealthyEver.com/book or scan the QR code below and get started.

PART 2

MULTIPLY

4

MULTIPLY – MULTIPLY YOUR WEALTH THROUGH INVESTMENTS

I began my engineering career, earning real money for the first time. I had a stable salary and contributed to a company-sponsored 401 (k) retirement account, so I thought I was set for the future. After some time, I reconsidered my future paths, applied to law school, and was accepted.

It seemed reasonable to assume that a lawyer would earn even more money, and I could save for retirement later. I told myself, "I have plenty of time to catch up." I didn't realize I was missing out on something much bigger: decades of compound interest. The money I didn't invest early in my career wouldn't just cost me the amount I could have saved, it would cost me the *growth* that money could have generated over a lifetime. That's the magic of compounding interest, and I was overlooking it.

My big mistake was believing that one day, wealth would materialize, that it was something' "future me" could manage. It took me years to enhance my financial habits, automate my savings and investments, and establish a system that worked for my family and me. Once I did, I was on my way towards my wealthy ever after.

This chapter emphasizes reshaping your view of money to transform your life, just as it transformed mine.

Introduction to Multiplying Wealth

Here's a question: What if your money could go out into the world and work for you, like an employee, even while you sleep? It sounds amazing, right? That's the concept behind multiplying wealth. It's not just about earning more at your job; it's about making the money you already have grow and work for you, just like an employee.

In the last chapter, we explored the importance of building multiple income streams, including passive ones. This chapter and the next will take it further by focusing on multiplying those income streams, allowing your wealth to grow impressively.

This concept is the second wealth accelerator commonly used by prosperous people. Achieving lasting financial freedom requires more than hard work and saving. It involves creating a system where your money works for you, generating passive income that grows.

- Active Income: Money you earn through work. Whether you're clocking in, freelancing, or managing a business, your efforts directly result in earnings. However, the moment you stop working, the income stops.
- Passive Income: Income doesn't require constant effort: investments, rental properties, or owning a business that operates independently. Your money works in the background, growing while you sleep.

If you want the freedom to step back from relentless work someday, shift your mindset. Instead of asking, "How can I earn more now?", ask, "How can I make my money multiply?" This mental shift is crucial because, with the right strategy, building wealth begins to feel not only possible but also inevitable.

In this chapter, we will discuss the concepts and basics of financial investing, which we will expand upon in Chapter 5 with investing tactics.

Financial Investing Basics

It's one thing to want your money to grow, but how do you make it happen? Don't worry, it's simpler than it sounds. Understanding a few key concepts will help you develop a multiplying mindset.

The Rule of 72

This is one of the simplest yet fascinating math tricks you'll discover for estimating how quickly your money can double. Here's how it works:

Take the number 72 and divide it by your investment's expected annual return (or interest rate). The result will estimate the years it takes for your money to double.

For instance, if your investment yields a 6% annual return, divide 72 by 6. This gives you 12, meaning your money will double in 12 years. If you earn 8%, it doubles even faster, divide 72 by 8, it will double in just 9 years!

Imagine investing $5,000 at an 8% return. After 9 years, you will have $10,000. If you leave it invested, it will double again to $20,000 in another 9 years, without you having to touch it. Pretty amazing, right?

The Rule of 72 demonstrates that the earlier you begin investing, the more time you allow your money to work for you. Additionally, the longer it works, the larger it grows.

Annual Interest Rate	Rule of 72	Actual Number of Years
1%	72	69.66
2%	36	35
3%	24	23.45
4%	18	17.67
5%	14.4	14.21
10%	7.2	7.27
20%	3.6	3.8
30%	2.4	2.64
50%	1.44	1.71

**Saving vs. Gambling vs. Trading vs. Investing:
Understanding the Risks and Rewards**

Once you start to think about growing your money, you'll encounter a few different ways. Not all of them are smart. Here's a quick breakdown of the four main ones and why investing wins.

1. Saving
   » Saving involves placing your money in a savings account or another secure location. It carries low risk and is ideal for emergencies. However, the downside is that it grows slowly. Most traditional savings accounts yield only pennies and do not keep pace with inflation, decreasing your money's value over time. High-yield Savings Accounts provide an interest rate of 3-5%. A high-yield savings account is a good option for storing your opportunity fund.

2. Gambling
   » Gambling involves taking significant risks to win big, such as purchasing lottery tickets or betting on sports. It may sound thrilling, but the odds are rarely in your favor. Most gamblers end up losing more than they win.
   The "house" always wins.

3. Trading
   » Trading involves swiftly buying and selling stocks or other investments to generate a profit. It demands skill, time, and considerable attention to the market. For beginners, it often resembles gambling - it's all too easy to lose money quickly.

4. Investing
   » Investing is a smart and steady way to grow your money by putting it into investments that appreciate over time, such as stocks, funds, real estate, and businesses. Unlike gambling or trading, investing emphasizes long-term growth rather than quick wins.
   Gambling is risky and unpredictable, while trading is hard work and not gentle for beginners. Saving is safe but slow. On the other hand, investing gives you the best chance to grow your money steadily over the years.

Avoiding the Gambling Trap

Sometimes, it's easy to confuse gambling with investing. If you're pursuing the hottest stock, jumping into a trendy cryptocurrency, or seeking anything appealing to "get rich quick," you might be gambling.

Here's the key difference: Investing involves making thoughtful, informed decisions regarding assets that appreciate over time, it's not about luck or hype. If you're taking a significant risk, step back, conduct your research, and ask yourself, "Am I truly investing?"

By grasping these simple concepts, how your money can double with the Rule of 72 and why investing is preferable to saving or gambling, you're already on your path to thinking like an investor. When you concentrate on growing your money effectively, your wealth doesn't merely accumulate, it multiplies. And that's how you transition from working for money to having your money work for you.

Investing in Appreciating Assets

Imagine planting a small seed today and watching it develop into a big, sturdy tree over time. That's what investing in appreciating assets is like, investing your money in things that increase in value as the years pass.

Appreciating assets include stocks, which represent small ownership in companies; real estate, such as homes or rental properties; and businesses, whether it's a consulting business you start or shares in an established company. These tend to gain value over time, especially if you hold onto them.

The real magic occurs with *compounding returns*. This is when your money earns money, and those earnings also begin to generate additional income! For example, if you invest $1,000 and it grows by 8% in a year, you'll have $1,080. The following year, instead of only earning 8% on your initial $1,000, you also earn on that extra $80 you made. Over time, this accumulates into something significant.

Consistent investing, even in small amounts, fosters growth. Think of it like building a snowman. Initially, you roll a tiny snowball, but it grows larger as it collects more snow. That's how wealth accumulates with steady, small investments.

One common mistake people make is trying to time the market. They attempt to buy at the ideal moment and sell at the right time. Unfortunately, even the best investors occasionally miss their mark. Instead of attempting to outsmart the market, spend as much *time in the market* as possible. Starting early and remaining invested is the most reliable way to see your money grow, no crystal ball needed!

The Role of Smart Leverage

What if you could use tools to enhance your earning potential, like adding rocket fuel to your wealth-building strategy? That's where *leverage* comes in. In straightforward terms, leverage means borrowing money to invest, and when utilized wisely, it can help you accelerate your wealth growth.

Here's an example: suppose you want to buy a house worth $200,000, but you only have $40,000 saved. A mortgage allows you to purchase a house by borrowing the remaining amount from the bank. Over time, as real estate prices rise, the home's value increases, and your initial investment (the $40,000) grows even more because you've leveraged it.

Here's another example. Suppose you run a small cleaning company. You have a solid customer base but can only manage several clients with your current equipment and staff. If you borrow money to hire additional cleaners or purchase better tools, like a professional-grade floor polisher or upholstery cleaner, you could take on more jobs and increase your profits. Over time, the extra income you earn could outweigh the cost of the loan, enabling your business to grow faster than it could have without that investment.

Leverage can multiply your returns, but here's an important warning: *too much leverage introduces risks*. Borrowing excessively can leave you overexposed, which means you'll struggle if things don't go as planned. To manage these risks, always borrow within limits you're comfortable repaying and focus on smart, reliable investments rather than risky, speculative ones. Think of leverage as a powerful tool, use it carefully, and it can create amazing results.

The Mindset Shift

You must think like an investor instead of a spender to multiply your wealth. Rather than concentrating solely on what money can buy today (clothes, gadgets, or vacations), focus on how money can grow for you in the future.

For many people, fear represents a significant hurdle. Risk can feel daunting, and the possibility of losing money may prevent you from even attempting. Alternatively, you might find yourself overthinking every decision, resulting in *analysis paralysis*, being stuck and taking no action whatsoever.

Analysis Paralysis:

THE THINKER   **THE OVERTHINKER**

To overcome this, focus on the bigger picture. Ask yourself, "What are my goals for the next 5, 10, or 20 years?" Start small, build your confidence, and remember that no investment plan is perfect. What matters most is getting started.

Patience and consistency are your best allies. Wealth does not grow overnight, it develops year by year. Most successful investors approach it as a long-term endeavor, remaining consistent even when the markets become volatile. It's akin to planting a garden. You water and nurture it regularly; you will enjoy a harvest over time.

Finally, build habits that support your new mindset. Here are a few examples:

- Automate your investments to grow your wealth without needing your constant attention.
- Concentrate on understanding money through reading books, watching videos, or consulting trusted advisors.
- Avoid emotional spending by taking a day or two before making big purchases.

Changing your habits takes time, but everything else falls into place once you shift this mindset. By multiplying your wealth, you're building money and freedom for yourself and your family.

Investing in appreciating assets, using leverage wisely, and shifting your mindset to focus on growth sets you up for a future where money doesn't control you, you are in control!

Start now and watch your wealth grow.

A Sneak Peek at Chapter 5

Before we wrap up, get ready to unlock the next game-changing step in your wealth-building journey. Chapter 5 dives into the powerful systems that can take your financial growth to the next level.

Imagine a world where your financial goals practically manage themselves. You'll discover how to establish systems that automate your savings, investments, and even bill payments, freeing you from the mental burden of managing money.

Here's what's in store:

- The step-by-step process to automate your finances, ensuring steady progress toward your financial goals without a second thought.
- How to utilize tax-advantaged accounts such as 401(k)s, IRAs, and other tools to accelerate wealth growth.
- Tips for scaling your investments and consistently building, even during life's busiest moments.

By the end of Chapter 5, you'll understand how to put your finances on autopilot and establish a system that works for you around the clock. Stay tuned to learn how to make your money work harder so you can focus on living the life you love!

5

MULTIPLY YOUR WEALTH – AUTOMATE YOUR INVESTMENTS AND INVEST IN STOCKS, REAL ESTATE, AND ALTERNATIVE INVESTMENTS

How the Wealthy Invest Differently—and How You Can Too

One of my wealthiest clients had an approach, and a portfolio, that completely changed my perspective about wealth-building.

I had worked with high-earning professionals and business owners for years, people making seven or eight figures. Yet many of them still felt financially overwhelmed. They were investing in stocks, maxing out their retirement accounts, and following all the "right" financial advice, but they were disappointed. Their wealth wasn't growing as they had expected or hoped.

Then I met this client. She wasn't just investing in the stock market, her portfolio was stacked with diversified assets, including stocks, real estate syndications, private investments, and alternative assets.

She explained, "Wealth isn't just about making money, it's about putting the right pieces together. You must grow your money, multiply it, and minimize taxes."

That was her investment puzzle, and it was a game changer.

Most people focus on just one or two pieces of the puzzle:

- They invest in stocks - but don't diversify beyond the market.
- They make high incomes - but don't minimize their taxes.
- They try to grow wealth but dedicate so much time and attention that they lose focus on what they want to do and get disappointing results.

The wealthy think differently. They don't invest in just one thing, they build portfolios that grow, multiply, and protect their wealth.

I suddenly realized: Building wealth isn't just about investing. It's about putting together the full investment puzzle.

- GROW — Learn how to manage money, increase income, and take control of your finances.
- MULTIPLY — Invest strategically in stocks, real estate, and alternative assets to build true wealth.
- PROTECT — Minimize taxes and legal risks to ensure wealth lasts for generations.

This chapter is about Wealth Accelerator #2: Multiply, investing in a way that builds lasting wealth.

Yes, we'll talk about minimizing taxes, but we'll go deeper into that in Chapter 8. For now, know that investing isn't just about returns, it's about structuring your portfolio so you keep more of what you earn.

For stock market basics, see the Appendix: Investing 101.

SECTION A: AUTOMATING WEALTH—HOW THE RICH INVEST WITHOUT THINKING ABOUT IT

Most people invest inconsistently. They put money into the market when they "remember" or think it's the right time. But the wealthy don't guess and don't rely merely on willpower. They automate their investments, so their money grows on autopilot. This isn't just about convenience, it's about removing emotion from investing. The market goes up and down, but the people who automate their investments win over time.

Investing is like brushing your teeth. You don't decide whether to do it each morning, you do it. The wealthy treat investing the same way.

Step 1: Maximize Tax-Advantaged Accounts First

The wealthy prioritize tax-advantaged accounts before investing in anything else because keeping more of your money is just as important as growing it.

- Employer-Sponsored Retirement Plans (401k, Roth 401k) — Contribute at least enough to get your company's match (it's free money). Then, aim to max out your contributions each year.
- Roth IRA — Tax-free growth and withdrawals in retirement. If you qualify, this should be a priority.
- Health Savings Account (HSA) — If you have a high-deductible health plan, this is a triple-tax-advantaged investment account: tax-free contributions, tax-free growth, and tax-free withdrawals for medical expenses.
- 529 Plans — Ideal for growing tax-free education savings for children. Moreover, if the funds aren't used for their education, up to $35,000 can be rolled into a Roth IRA for your child's retirement.
- Self-Directed IRAs (SDIRA) — For those who want to invest in real estate or private equity with tax advantages.

Once these tax-advantaged accounts are funded, you can diversify into stocks, real estate, and alternative assets.

Step 2: Automate Stock Investments for Long-Term Growth

Many people with a range of incomes, including the wealthiest people in the world, own stocks. Warren Buffett, Jeff Bezos, and other billionaires all have significant portions of their portfolios in the stock market.

Instead of trying to time the market, the wealthy set up automatic contributions to stock investments.

The best ways to automate stock investing:

- Index Funds & ETFs — A simple, diversified investment method without picking individual stocks.
- Dividend Stocks — These stocks pay out passive income while appreciating over time.
- Target-Date Funds — A hands-off investment method based on when you plan to retire.

The key? Consistency beats timing. Even if the market drops, automated investments ensure you're buying at lower prices and benefiting from long-term growth.

For stock market investing strategies, see the Appendix: Investing 101.

Step 3: Automate Contributions to Real Estate & Alternative Investments

The wealthy don't just invest in stocks. They also allocate money to real estate, private businesses, and other alternative assets automatically. These investments include:

- Real Estate Investment Trusts (REITs) — Publicly traded real estate investments that provide cash flow.
- Real Estate Syndications & Funds — Passive investments in large-scale real estate projects.
- Private Equity & Venture Capital — Invest in private businesses before they go public.
- Private Lending — Becoming the bank and earning passive interest.

Setting up automatic transfers into these investments removes decision fatigue and builds wealth without constant effort.

Step 4: Reinvest Returns Instead of Pulling Profits Too Early

The final key to automated investing is not interrupting the compounding process.

Many investors make the mistake of pulling out profits too soon. The wealthy let their investments grow, reinvesting dividends, interest, and cash flow to create exponential returns.

- Dividends should be reinvested into more shares.
- Real estate cash flow can be reinvested into more properties or alternative assets.
- Stock market gains can be left alone to compound over time.

The longer your money stays invested, the harder it works for you.

The Wealthy Invest on Autopilot—You Can Too

A big difference between the wealthy and everyone else isn't just how much they invest, it's how consistently they invest. By automating contributions, prioritizing tax advantages, diversifying across stocks and alternative assets, and reinvesting returns, you're building a system that multiplies wealth while you sleep.

SECTION B: INVESTING IN STOCKS AND BEYOND

Why Stocks Are a Core Part of a Wealth Strategy

When many people think of investing, they think of the stock market, for good reason. Stocks have historically been one of the greatest long-term wealth-building tools, providing compound growth, passive income through dividends, and diversification across industries and global markets.

The wealthy understand that stocks are a critical piece of the investment puzzle, but they don't stop there. They combine stock market investments with other assets to build a balanced, diversified portfolio that grows in all market conditions.

If investing in stocks feels overwhelming, check out the Appendix: Investing 101 for a breakdown of stocks, bonds, and ETFs and instructions on how to get started.

How the Wealthy Invest in Stocks

Instead of chasing "hot" stocks or day trading, the wealthy generally take a systematic, diversified approach to stock investing. Here's how:

1. Core Stock Market Strategy: Index Funds & ETFs

Most high-net-worth investors build their stock portfolio around index funds and ETFs (exchange-traded funds). These funds provide instant diversification, meaning you don't have to pick individual stocks to succeed.

- S&P 500 Index Funds: Invests in the 500 largest U.S. companies, offering long-term growth.
- Total Market ETFs: Provides exposure to the entire U.S. stock market.
- International ETFs: Diversifies into global markets to reduce risk.

Why this works: Passive investing outperforms active stock picking over time. Instead of constantly monitoring the market, index funds let your money grow with the economy.

2. Dividend Stocks: Getting Paid While You Invest

Dividend stocks pay you regularly, even if the market fluctuates. Investors hold dividend-paying companies for consistent income and reinvest the dividends to accelerate growth.

- Blue-chip dividend stocks: Large, established companies with a history of paying dividends (Coca-Cola, Johnson & Johnson, Procter & Gamble). Some of these stocks are referred to as Dividend Aristocrats.

- Dividend ETFs: Baskets of dividend-paying stocks for automatic diversification.

A smart strategy is reinvesting dividends instead of cashing them out, this compounds wealth over time.

Global Investing for Diversification

While the U.S. market has been a strong performer, international investments provide diversification, hedge against currency risks, and expose you to high-growth economies.

Ways to invest internationally:

- Foreign Index Funds & ETFs: Funds that track Europe, Asia, or emerging markets.
- Global Real Estate: Investing in international properties or real estate funds.
- Offshore Investment Accounts: Legally structured accounts that optimize tax efficiency.

The goal isn't to replace U.S. stock investments but to diversify globally so your wealth isn't dependent on just one economy.

Stocks as a Foundation—Not the Whole Strategy

The wealthy don't put all their eggs in one basket. They use stocks as the foundation of their portfolio while adding real estate, private investments, and alternative assets for greater security and growth.

SECTION C: INVESTING IN REAL ESTATE AND ALTERNATIVE ASSETS

Why the Wealthy Invest Beyond Stocks

The stock market is a powerful wealth-building tool, but the truly wealthy don't stop there. They diversify into real estate, private businesses, and alternative investments to reduce risk, increase cash flow, and hedge against market volatility.

Unlike stocks, which fluctuate daily, these investments provide stability, tax advantages, and passive income. This is why real estate moguls, billionaires, and family offices allocate large portions of their wealth outside the public markets.

Here's how you can do the same.

Investing in Real Estate: A Key Wealth Multiplier

Real estate has been one of the most consistent wealth-building assets for generations. It provides appreciation, cash flow, and tax benefits that stocks alone can't offer.

1. Rental Properties: Generating Passive Income

Owning rental properties allows you to earn monthly cash flow while building long-term equity. Over time, rents increase, mortgages get paid down, and properties appreciate.

Best options for beginners:

- Single-family rentals (SFRs): Easier to manage, great for beginners.
- Multifamily properties (duplexes, triplexes, apartment buildings): Higher income potential, but more complicated to manage.

2. Real Estate Investment Trusts (REITs): Own Real Estate Without the Hassle

A REIT is like a stock that invests in real estate. It allows you to own a share of income-generating properties without managing tenants or buildings.

- Public REITs: Traded on the stock market, providing liquidity and dividends.
- Private REITs: Available to accredited investors, often with higher returns.

REITs are a great option for hands-off real estate investing while benefiting from rental income and property appreciation.

3. Real Estate Syndications & Funds: Investing in Large-Scale Deals

A real estate syndication pools money from multiple investors to buy properties like apartment buildings, commercial real estate, or developments.

- Why it's powerful: You get the benefits of real estate ownership without actively managing properties.
- How to invest: Join syndications through real estate investment platforms or private investor networks.

This is how the ultra-wealthy invest in real estate without dealing with tenants, maintenance, or property management.

Alternative Investments: Expanding Beyond Real Estate

The wealthy don't just rely on real estate and stocks, they diversify into private investments, lending, and alternative assets that grow wealth uniquely.

1. Private Lending: Becoming the Bank

Instead of taking out loans, the wealthy lend money and collect interest. Private lending allows you to earn passive income by financing real estate deals, small businesses, or personal loans.

Ways to invest in private lending:

- Hard money loans: Short-term real estate loans with high interest rates.
- Peer-to-peer lending platforms: Lending directly to individuals and businesses.
- Seller financing: Structuring deals where you finance real estate buyers instead of a bank.

Lenders earn predictable, passive returns while maintaining control over their investments.

2. Private Equity & Venture Capital: Investing in Businesses Before They Go Public

Wealthy investors don't just buy stocks, they own pieces of private businesses through private equity and venture capital.

How to access private business investments:

- Angel Investing: Providing early-stage funding to startups in exchange for equity.
- Private Equity Funds: Investing in established private businesses with growth potential.
- Franchise Ownership: Owning a share in profitable business models with proven track records.

Investing in private companies can produce strong returns when businesses grow, get acquired, or go public.

3. Collectibles, Art, and Alternative Assets

Many high-net-worth investors allocate a portion of their wealth to alternative assets like fine art, wine, collectibles, and digital assets like cryptocurrency.

- Why? These assets are often independent of the stock market and can hold or increase in value over time.
- How to invest: Platforms now allow fractional ownership of collectibles, making them accessible to more investors.

These investments aren't for everyone but provide unique opportunities to store and grow wealth outside traditional markets. They are considered quite risky because it is difficult to judge the worth of collectibles and art where the price follows the demand, and demand can be inconsistent. For example, there was a time when stamp collecting was booming, and rare stamps were quite valuable due to the high demand. When stamp collecting became less popular, demand decreased, and the value of the same stamps decreased as well.

Expanding Beyond the U.S.: The Case for International Investing

Many investors focus only on U.S. markets, but global investing provides additional diversification, hedging against currency fluctuations, and access to high-growth economies.

Ways to invest internationally:

- Global Real Estate: Buying rental properties or REITs in high-growth foreign markets.
- Foreign Index Funds & ETFs: Investing in emerging markets and international companies.
- Offshore Investment Accounts: Legally structured accounts that optimize tax efficiency.

Adding international investments to your portfolio reduces risk and increases opportunities for long-term wealth growth.

The Wealthy Don't Rely on One Investment—They Build a Portfolio That Works in Any Market

By combining stocks, real estate, private investments, and global diversification, you create a wealth strategy that grows regardless of economic conditions.

SECTION D: INVESTING FOR CHILDREN— CREATING GENERATIONAL WEALTH

Why the Wealthy Invest for Their Kids Early

The biggest advantage in investing isn't just how much you invest and how early you start investing. Wealthy families understand that time is the most powerful tool in wealth-building, so they set up investment accounts for their children as soon as possible.

While most parents focus on college savings, the wealthy go beyond education savings. They invest in ways that help their kids build long-term wealth, financial literacy, and ownership from an early age.

Here's how you can do the same.

Best Investment Accounts for Kids

1. Custodial Roth IRA: The Ultimate Wealth Tool for Kids

A Custodial Roth IRA allows kids with earned income to invest for retirement completely tax-free. This is one of the most powerful accounts for building generational wealth because:

- Contributions grow tax-free and can be withdrawn tax-free in retirement.
- It teaches kids the power of investing early.
- A small investment in their teenage years can grow into millions over time.

How to qualify: Your child must have earned income from a part-time job, business, or even modeling for your business.

For business owners, one of the best ways to qualify is by putting your kids on the payroll. See the Kids on Payroll Class in the Law Mother app for more details.

How to invest: Set up automatic contributions into index funds, ETFs, or dividend stocks.

A $6,000 investment at age 15 could grow into over $1 million by retirement, even without adding more money.

2. 529 Plans: Tax-Free Education Investing

A 529 Plan is one of the best ways to save for college because:

- Money grows tax-free and can be withdrawn tax-free for education expenses.
- Some states offer tax deductions for contributions.
- Under the SECURE Act 2.0, if a child doesn't use all the funds for school, up to $35,000 can be rolled into their Roth IRA.

How to maximize: Invest in a low-cost index fund within the 529 plan for long-term growth.

Family members can contribute, making it a great gift. Toys may delight the child for a short while and then be put away forever, but contributions are an investment that will benefit the child forever.

3. UTMA/UGMA Accounts: A Flexible Investment Account for Kids

A Uniform Transfer to Minors Account (UTMA/UGMA) allows parents to invest money for their kids in stocks, ETFs, and even real estate.

- Unlike a 529 plan, funds can be used for anything, not just education.
- Depending on the state, the child gains full account control at age 18 or 21.

Best for: Parents who want to give kids a jumpstart on wealth without restrictions.

The downside is that once the child gains control, they can use the money however they want. Teaching financial literacy is key here. Alternatively, many clients invest for their children in a brokerage account in their own (the parent's) name and later earmark the money for the children.

How the Wealthy Teach Kids to Invest

Setting up accounts is one thing, but teaching kids investing creates generational wealth.

1. Let Kids Pick Stocks They Know

When kids get excited about investing, they engage more. A great way to start is by letting them invest in brands they love, Disney, Nike, Apple, etc.

How to do it:

- Open a custodial brokerage account.
- Let them research companies and buy a few shares.
- Show them how stock prices move over time.

This builds financial literacy and ownership at an early age.

2. Introduce Real Estate Investing

Many wealthy families buy rental properties for their children so they can start earning passive income early.

How to do it:

- Buy a small rental property and have the rent fund their investment accounts.
- Involve kids in the process, teach them how to analyze deals, calculate returns, and manage properties.
- When they turn 18, transfer the property to them as a long-term asset.

This gives them an appreciating asset and passive income for life.

3. Encourage Entrepreneurship & Ownership

Many wealthy families teach their kids to make money in addition to saving it.

How to do it:

- Help them start a small business (Etsy store, tutoring, lawn care, etc.).
- Show them how to invest their profits instead of just spending them.
- Introduce them to private investments, angel investing, real estate, or crowdfunding.

As they graduate high school, they will understand how money works, how to invest, and how to build assets. This education will serve them well throughout their lives.

The Power of Starting Early

Most people start investing in their 30s or 40s. By setting up investments for your children now, you give them a multi-decade head start.

Wealthy families don't just pass down money, they pass down knowledge, habits, and investment strategies.

SECTION E: SCALING AND PROTECTING YOUR INVESTMENTS

Why Scaling Your Investments Matters

Building wealth isn't just about making investments, it's about scaling them over time so your money works harder for you. The wealthy don't stop at simply investing; they continually optimize, reinvest, and protect their assets to ensure long-term financial growth.

This section will cover how to:

- Expand your investments strategically as your wealth grows.
- Use reinvestment to accelerate compounding.
- Protect what you've built so it lasts for generations.

Step 1: Expanding Investments Over Time

As your financial situation improves, your investment strategy should evolve. The key is shifting from accumulation to optimization, moving from simple investing to building a portfolio that maximizes returns while minimizing risk.

Here's how the wealthy expand their investments over time:

Increase Contributions to Existing Investments

Once your income grows, increasing contributions to stocks, real estate, and alternative investments helps compound wealth even faster.

- Max out tax-advantaged accounts (401k, Roth IRA, HSA, 529).
- Increase automatic investments in index funds and ETFs.
- Buy additional rental properties or expand into syndications.

Diversify Into More Alternative Investments

Beyond stocks and real estate, the next step is exploring higher-return investments like:

- Private Equity & Venture Capital—Investing in businesses before they go public.
- Private Lending—Becoming the bank and earning passive income.
- Global Investments—Expanding into international real estate and markets.

As wealth increases, diversification protects against economic downturns, while expanding growth opportunities.

Step 2: Using Reinvestment to Accelerate Wealth Growth

One of the biggest differences between the wealthy and average investors is how they use their investment returns.

Instead of withdrawing gains, the wealthy reinvest profits to maximize compounding.

Here's how to reinvest effectively:

- Reinvest Dividends—Instead of cashing out, allow dividends to buy more shares automatically.
- Recycle Real Estate Cash Flow—Use rental income to acquire more properties.
- Compound Returns in Alternative Investments—Roll over gains from private equity and lending into new opportunities.

This strategy turns one investment into multiple wealth-building assets over time.

Step 3: Protect Your Wealth from Losses
(we'll discuss this in detail in Part 3).

Making money is one thing, keeping it is another. Wealthy individuals don't just focus on investing; they also structure their assets to reduce risk, limit taxes, and create long-term security.

Asset Protection Strategies

To shield investments from lawsuits, creditors, or unexpected risks, high-net-worth individuals use:

- LLCs & Trusts—Holding assets in business entities or trusts can provide legal protection.
- Umbrella Insurance—Extra liability coverage to safeguard wealth.
- Estate Planning—Ensuring investments pass to heirs without costly legal battles.

These strategies ensure that wealth doesn't disappear due to lawsuits, taxes, or financial mismanagement.

Tax Planning for Investors

One of the wealthiest investors' biggest advantages is understanding tax efficiency.

Strategies include:

- 1031 Exchanges—Deferring capital gains taxes on real estate by reinvesting in new properties.
- Tax-Loss Harvesting—Using stock market losses to offset capital gains.
- Charitable Giving Strategies—Donating stocks or assets for tax deductions.

For a deeper dive into tax strategies, see Chapter 8: Protecting Your Wealth from Taxes.

FINAL THOUGHTS: THE WEALTH CYCLE NEVER STOPS

Scaling and protecting investments are what separates temporary wealth from lasting wealth. The wealthy invest, reinvest, and protect, on repeat. By following these steps, you're not just investing for today, you're building a wealth strategy that grows and lasts for generations.

Call to Action: Your Next Steps

Now that you understand how to invest like the wealthy, it's time to act. Building wealth doesn't happen overnight, but small, consistent steps yield massive results over time.

Here's how to get started:

1. Automate your investments.
   - » Set up automatic contributions to your retirement accounts, brokerage accounts, and alternative investments.
   - » Remove decision fatigue by making investing a habit, not a choice.

2. Diversify beyond just stocks.
    »   While stocks are essential to wealth-building, the wealthy don't rely on a single asset class.
    »   Expand into real estate, private equity, and alternative investments to create a well-rounded portfolio.
3. Explore an alternative investment this year.
    »   If you've only invested in stocks, now is the time to add real estate, private lending, or another alternative asset to your strategy.
    »   Start small and build from there, the key is acting.
4. Track your investments.
    »   Stay on your wealth-building journey with tools to help you set goals, automate investments, and track progress.

APPENDIX: INVESTING 101 (FOR THOSE WHO NEED IT)

If you're new to investing or want a refresher, check out the Investing 101 Appendix, where you'll find:

*   A breakdown of stocks, bonds, ETFs, and index funds.
*   How to start investing even if you're a beginner.
*   Strategies to build a diversified portfolio that aligns with your financial goals.

No matter where you are in your wealth-building journey, the key is to start and stay consistent. The best investors aren't the ones who time the market perfectly, they're the ones who stay in the game.

PART 3

PROTECT

6

PROTECT: ESTATE PLANNING

My husband and I sat in the movie theater on a date night, waiting for the show to start. He asked me what would happen to our daughter if we didn't make it home safely that night and hadn't put an estate plan in place. We live in Colorado, and all our relatives live thousands of miles away, in Arizona, California, and Iowa. If we hadn't established an estate plan and didn't return home, our babysitter would contact the police, who would then notify Child Protective Services. Child protective services would arrive at our house, and a stranger would take our daughter from our home to a foster home.

That would be very scary for our daughter.

Our parents and siblings would travel to Colorado, find and hire lawyers, and request a court case. During the court case, a judge would listen to both my parents and my husband's parents to decide who would care for our daughter. We might hope our families would get along, but they might disagree on who should raise our kids. As parents, this situation is unsettling and downright scary! Unfortunately, many families do not have an estate plan. As a former Deputy District Attorney, I have seen this situation arise repeatedly. An accident happens, and Child Protective Services or foster care takes their children during the legal process. Those families were without the legal planning tools described in this book.

Thankfully, we have an estate plan and revisit it every three years.

But this isn't just our story. Think about Cinderella. Growing up, my parents read me the story of Cinderella, an orphan mistreated by her evil stepmother and stepsisters. Cinderella's happily ever after starts with the help of her fairy godmother and ends with her in the arms of a prince.

Thinking about the story today as a mom and a lawyer, I consider an alternative option: a legally happy ever after that starts with an estate plan and ends with Cinderella's protected inheritance and a loving caregiver. After all, Cinderella's parents would never have wanted their daughter to lose everything and become a servant in her own home.

This chapter focuses on taking control of your legacy to protect yourself and your loved ones. Whether you're beginning your estate planning journey or seeking to enhance an existing plan, this is your opportunity to create a future where your voice, values, and vision shape what you leave behind.

In real life, happily-ever-after isn't just a fairy tale. It's a choice, and it starts with planning.

To dive deeper into estate planning, download the FREE Law Mother App. You'll get a free copy of my bestselling book, Legally Ever After, to discover the 6-step plan to protect your children and future. You'll also get access to additional estate planning attorneys, tools and videos designed to guide you every step of the way. This app is your gateway to actionable steps that simplify the process and empower you to secure what matters most.

What is estate planning, exactly?

In simple terms, estate planning is the process of ensuring that your wishes are fulfilled for you and your family if something happens to you.

With proper estate planning, a fairy godmother isn't needed to facilitate a meaningful transfer of assets to your loved ones and ensure their care. In other words, if Cinderella's family had developed an estate plan, she would have had the opportunity to process her grief over losing both parents and would not have also had to suffer the loss of her childhood home.

While the Cinderella story may have been fictional, there are many young and adult children all over the world who are being taken advantage of like Cinderella. These families did not properly plan their estate before they died, causing their own children to be deprived of what is rightfully theirs in an inheritance.

MYTHS ABOUT ESTATE PLANNING

Myth One: If I Prepare a Plan, Something Will Happen to Me

I understand this fear, and I hear this a lot from my clients, this idea that if I put an estate plan in place, something will happen to me. I will die unexpectedly. The good news is that of the thousands of cases I've worked on, I've seen no type of correlation or connection between putting an estate plan in place, and then something happening accidentally or suddenly.

The reality is that we will all pass on at some point. When the time comes, your loved ones will appreciate you taking the time now to get all your ducks in a row. Unfortunately, the alternative, doing nothing, will often result in your family going through the probate process, which is time-consuming and costly.

Myth Two: I Am Too Young to Plan

I get asked a lot of questions, am I too young to put together an estate plan? The answer is no. There isn't a set age and there's a common myth that you must be elderly to have an estate plan in place. Really, procrastination doesn't serve people well, considering the risk that something unexpected can happen any time - perhaps too late. Additionally, when people wait until they are unhealthy to put a plan in place, they often aren't making the best decisions.

LIFE EVENT CHECKLIST: WHEN SHOULD YOU UPDATE OR CREATE YOUR ESTATE PLAN?

The following checklist guides you on when you should create or update your estate plan based on life events.

Your Life Event Checklist

Have any of these events happened to you this year?

If you check one or more boxes below, it's time to update or create your estate plan.

- You reviewed your estate plan 5+ years ago
- Birth of first child, or children have turned 18 (or older)
- Got Married
- Got Divorced or remarried
- Individuals previously named are no longer appropriate
- Moved to a different state/relocated to or from a different state
- Have had a significant increase/decrease in the value of your assets
- Bought a vacation home or rental property
- Changed your primary residence
- You have an IRA, 401(k), or other qualified plan that requires you to begin to take distributions.

Myth Three: I Am Not Wealthy Enough to Plan

Dave and Naomi

Dave and Naomi are a young married couple with two kids under the age of ten. They are an average middle-class couple; they own a home and are saving up for their future. Dave's brother and dad are drug addicts. Dave and Naomi have sizeable life insurance plans and fear that if they were to die, Dave's brother and dad would try and get custody of their children. We put together a comprehensive estate plan to ensure that Dave and Naomi's assets and children are fully protected and kept out of the hands of their drug-addicted family members.

It's not about how much money you have; it's about how much input you want to have.

Without an estate plan, you are at the mercy of the government to make your decisions. Ultimately, a stranger, a judge will decide who will care for you financially and medically if you become disabled. The reality is most of us will be disabled some time in our life. Additionally, a judge will decide who will care for your kids if they are minors, and if your children are adults, they will receive their inheritance outright with no asset protection and without guidance.

Many people think they don't have enough money to pay for an estate plan. The reality is the cost of no plan is more than the cost of a plan. Probate court is the default plan if you do not have an estate plan. This is costly and inconvenient; on average it costs 5-9% of your estate and takes between 9 months and two years. For example, a family with a $400k home, $500,000 in life insurance and $100,000 in retirement accounts will lose $50,000-$90,000 in probate. Alternatively, by creating an estate plan with a qualified attorney, they will avoid the $50,000-$90,000 in probate costs and only pay the estate plan costs between $4,000-$6,000.

Myth Four: All I Need is a Simple Will

Many parents believe they only need a simple will to protect their loved ones. Unfortunately, a will alone is not enough. A won't cover what happens if you're incapacitated or disabled. A will must also go through the probate court, be filed with the court, and a lawsuit is commenced for a will to be effective.

What is probate?

Probate is a court proceeding. Each state has its own probate court process. During the probate process, a judge decides how assets are transferred.

When your family members or loved ones must go through probate to help you or your estate, they get a case number. There are court fees, legal fees, and you are reliant on the timetable of the courts. On average, the probate process takes 9 months to two years and costs 5-9% of your estate value.

The probate process also becomes involved if there is a minor child or incapacitated adult. The judge decides who will oversee the minor or incapacitated adult's financial affairs and medical decisions.

The probate court gets involved when you pass away or become incapacitated and have a will in place, or if you have no plan in place. However, you can create an estate plan that avoids probate.

If you haven't created an estate plan that will avoid probate, you're leaving it up to a probate judge to figure out who's in charge of your finances if you're incapacitated, and who becomes guardian of your children if something happens to you.

Myth Five: If I am Married My Spouse Will Automatically Be in Charge

If you are married, you still need a plan. Without one, your spouse will likely have to deal with frozen bank accounts when you pass away. They will have to go to court to be able to make decisions if you become disabled. Without a plan, your spouse will lose the opportunity to minimize the taxes paid and will not benefit from asset protection. Additionally, eventually both of you will die and some action must be taken with your remaining assets.

There is a common misconception that if you are ever incapacitated or disabled, your spouse will automatically be able to act on your behalf. However, this is not true.

The law does not assume that your spouse has your best interest. Therefore, absent a legal plan, your spouse would have to go to probate court to ask the judge to make your medical and financial decisions. If a family member wishes to make medical or financial decisions, for example, your parents or a sibling, they can ask the judge to appoint them as financial or medical guardians. One of the most famous examples of this is the Terri Schiavo case.

In the early morning of February 25, 1990, Terri Schiavo collapsed in the hallway of her St. Petersburg, Florida apartment. The cause of Terri's collapse was determined to be cardiac arrest. Losing oxygen to her brain during the time before being resuscitated caused damage to her brain. After two and a half months without improvement, her doctors changed her diagnosis to that of a persistent vegetative state. At this point, Terri was being kept alive by artificial means.

Initially, the court appointed her husband Michael as her legal guardian. In 1998, he petitioned the court to disconnect Terri's feeding tube. Terri's parents opposed the removal of her feeding tube. Because Terri had never formally expressed her wishes regarding end-of-life treatment, nor had she appointed an Agent to make decisions for her, an epic legal battle began that ripped her family apart. It tore apart not just a family, but the nation, too, as many people chose sides. The saddest part of all is it could have all been avoided if Terri Schiavo simply had executed an advance health directive before her collapse.

Core Pieces of an Estate Plan

Estate planning begins with key documents, and this section will guide you through the essentials, like a will, trust, power of attorney, and healthcare directives. These are the foundation of any solid estate plan. But estate planning isn't just about the paperwork; it's about creating a strategy that reflects your unique goals and adapts as your life and circumstances change. A well-rounded plan goes beyond drafting documents, it ensures they work together to protect your loved ones, provide clarity, and safeguard your legacy. By linking these pieces to a bigger picture, you create a plan that offers security and peace of mind for years to come.

Providing Economic Support for Your Family:
The Benefits of a Living Trust

A living trust is a legal document, or trust, created during an individual's lifetime, where a designated person, the trustee, is responsible for managing that individual's assets to benefit the eventual beneficiary.

If Cinderella's father had created a living trust and appointed a trustee for his money, Cinderella would have received money for health, education, maintenance and support, and she wouldn't have been forced to dress in rags. When she grew old enough, Cinderella's dad's trust could have specified that Cinderella receive money to be able to buy her own home, and she could have led a nice life with her Prince Charming.

What is the difference between a will and a trust?

	Living Trust	Will
Avoids Probate Costs	☑ Yes	No
Provide for your care during a disability	☑ Yes	No
Quickly Settled	☑ Yes	No
Leave property to minor children	☑ Yes	No
Keep privacy after death	☑ Yes	No
Protection from court challenges	☑ Yes	No
Asset Protection	☑ Yes	No
Minimize Estate Taxes	☑ Yes	No

A will is a legal document that expresses a person's last wishes. A will is triggered at the creator's death ("testator") and undergoes probate after the creator's death. Probate is the court proceeding your loved ones will have to go through if you die without a plan or with a will alone. The probate process can be costly, on average 5-9% of your estate. Additionally, the probate process is time-consuming. It would put your family through a court process that can take on average, between nine months and two years; during that time, your family would not have access to your assets. A will-based plan means your asset transfer will be public, because it is a public court process.

A living trust is also a legal document that transfers assets; it comes into effect during the creator's life. One of the primary advantages of a living trust is that there is no probate court, i.e., there is no court process. Avoiding the probate process saves time and money. A living trust also allows you to transfer your assets privately. Living trusts also give you the option to plan to legally reduce estate taxes and protect family assets from future creditors and divorces.

Additionally, living trusts allow for you to plan for your incapacity. If you were ever incapacitated and only had a will in place or nothing in place, your loved ones would have to go to court to get access to the money to take care of you, your family, and your affairs. However, with a living trust, the court process is avoided, and you state exactly who you would want to manage your affairs if you were incapacitated.

Who should create a will-based plan?

In trust-based planning, a pour-over will is usually created. In other words, people who have living trusts also have a will. A pour over will is created with the hopes it will never be used. A pour over will is a safety measure or stop gap. If the trust is properly funded, meaning the title and beneficiary designation for all your assets are properly transferred to your trust, then a pour-over will never be used. However, if at the time of your passing there is an asset that is outside your trust, the pour over will direct the court to transfer the asset to the trust.

Some people choose to do a will-based plan, never forming a trust. For example, in some states, if you have under a certain amount of assets (i.e. $75,000) the probate process is expedited and less costly. If you aren't sure whether you want or need or will versus a trust, contact a lawyer who practices in your state and understand what would happen to your family in both scenarios. Most lawyers have an affordable initial consultation and will spend the time educating you based on your specific needs.

GUIDANCE FOR FINANCIAL AND MEDICAL DECISIONS

What happens if I become incapacitated without a written plan?

If you're incapacitated or disabled and not able to speak for yourself or make and communicate your decisions, then your relatives and spouse will have to go to court and ask the judge for permission to make medical and financial decisions on your behalf. If there is a conflict, for example, your spouse wants to remove you from life support and your parents do not, then a judge will resolve this conflict.

A common misconception is that if you are incapacitated or disabled and you are married, then your spouse can automatically and exclusively act for you. Even though you're married, there is no presumption that your spouse has your best interest. They would be required to go to the probate court before making any decisions without a Power of Attorney or similar documentation on file, just like anyone else would need to if they intended to act on your behalf. Don't rely merely on the fact that you're married to assume that your spouse gets to do that automatically for you; don't rely just on a will to cover all your estate planning concerns.

Guidance for Medical Decisions - Living Will

A Living Will (also known as an advanced health care directive in some states) sometimes is mistaken for a Last Will. A Living Will applies while you're alive and guides your healthcare preferences. A Last Will gives guidance on your possessions and body after your passing. A Living Will clarifies at what time, after what number of days, would you want to be taken off life support. For example, you could specify you want to be on life support for seven days or seven years. It's completely up to you. The important thing is that you've thought about it and put it in writing so that if your family finds itself in the situation, they know your choices and can honor them.

Having a living will honors your choices and avoids conflict between family members.

Guidance for Medical Decisions - Medical Power of Attorney

A Medical Power of Attorney is a legal document used to appoint people to make medical decisions on your behalf if you cannot. We also know a Medical Power of Attorney as a Health Care Power of Attorney, Health Care Proxy, Durable Power of Attorney for Health Care, and Power of Attorney Medical. Your medical power of attorney will follow your Living Will; however, if there is a gray area, the appointed person will be tasked with making the final decision. Designating a medical power of attorney avoids conflict down the road, instead of a judge deciding, your medical power of attorney will decide.

Family members often disagree about these tough decisions without a plan in place. These disagreements cause families a lot of suffering and can ultimately result in expensive and lengthy court battles. However, much of the cost and conflict can be avoided with a plan in place.

Guidance for Financial Decisions - Power of attorney (POA)

A Power of Attorney (POA) is a legal document that allows someone you choose to act on your behalf for specific legal or financial matters. The document outlines exactly what they can do and sets limits based on your instructions or state laws.

A POA usually ends when the person who created it passes away. It can also end if that person becomes unable to make decisions unless it's a "durable" POA, which means it remains valid even if they become incapacitated.

The Way to Create a Legally Protected Plan

Family Business and Online Plans

Tim and his father ran a successful construction company together for many years. His 80-year-old father was ready to retire and pass on the business to Tim. One night, Tim and his father drafted estate planning documents online. A few years later, Tim's father passes away. The estate plan Tim's father drafted online fails. His father didn't properly execute the online plan. His father did not understand how to pass on the business correctly, and instead of passing it on to Tim, it was now split between Tim and his estranged and drug-addicted brother.

Tim contributed financially to purchase the business real estate holdings, which were titled in his father's name solely. Therefore, his brother now has a claim to them. For the next three years, Tim spends countless hours and hundreds of thousands of dollars in probate court battling with his estranged brother. Tim must take out a mortgage on his house to keep the business afloat. Tim's marriage became strained. He barely has any time to spend with his kids and he's gained weight from the stresses of the court process.

Tim comes to my office because he wants to put together an estate plan to ensure that the nightmare he went through with his brother won't ever happen again. In four short weeks, we put together a comprehensive and personalized plan to protect his children, keep them out of court, reduce taxes and eliminate the cost of probate.

Should you hire a lawyer to create a plan?

Several do-it-yourself templates and online resources help you create your own estate plan. Can you write your own estate plan? The simple answer is yes, you can write your own estate plan. However, the more important question is, should you write your own estate plan?

Many people feel tempted by the seemingly low cost of using an online legal document provider to create legal documents. However, doing so could result in your plan failing, not doing what you wanted it to do, and long-term costs for your loved ones.

Hiring an experienced lawyer to prepare your legal plan provides the following advantages:

1. An Estate planning lawyer will save you time, money, and energy, and avoid common mistakes.

    Estate planning is complicated. Working with a legal professional helps. Hiring an estate planning lawyer will reduce the stress of securing your assets. One misplaced signature or omitted word can invalidate your estate plan.

Common mistakes an estate planning lawyer can help you avoid include:

» Designating incorrect beneficiaries on life insurance and retirement accounts
» Not completing the process
» Inadvertently leaving people out
» Not including all your assets
» Improper execution of documents
» Improper or inadequate funding of trusts

An estate planning lawyer will prevent mistakes and ensure you and your loved ones are cared for the way you intend. A carefully created plan will also help you protect your family from unnecessary conflict down the road.

2. Counseling

The "Simple Plan"

A New Jersey woman just needed a seemingly simple plan. She owned a $300,000 house and a $300,000 bank account. She had two adult children. She drafted a simple will herself, giving her house to her son and the bank account to her daughter. After her death, her children discover her will and realize she spent down her bank account to pay her bills, so there's nothing left for her daughter. The son who gets the house feels sorry for his sister but believes his mom wanted him to have the house. The daughter believes that was not her mother's intent and sues her brother. If the New Jersey mom had had proper counseling and advice from a lawyer, the suit could have been avoided, and her wishes would have been properly expressed in a legally binding document.

An estate planning lawyer provides more than technical document expertise. They are a trusted advisor who provides guidance, support, and strategy.

For example, many parents struggle with deciding who they should designate as the ideal guardian for their child.

An experienced estate planning lawyer will help a couple sift through the various options and choose a guardian based on their specific needs and circumstances.

3. Save Money on Taxes

    Prince's unexpected death in 2016 resulted in numerous court cases. Prince died without any estate planning documents. Prince did not have a spouse or children and left behind half-brothers and half-sisters.

    The federal estate tax is 40 percent, and Minnesota imposes a top death rate of 16 percent. There is a potential that Prince's $300 million estate will be reduced to $162 million just from taxes. This does not include the costs of probate, lawyers, and litigation. Five years later, Prince's heirs still have not inherited a dime, and there are already over $13 million in attorneys' fees.

    With some planning, Prince could have taken steps to keep his family members out of court and conflict and reduce estate taxes. Prince generously donated to charities. By failing to have an estate plan in place to continue those charitable gifts, Prince's estate lost out on the tremendous tax savings and the government, rather than the charities he supported, will benefit financially.

    State and federal tax laws often change and have become complicated. Many states have adopted their own estate tax structures.

    A qualified estate planning lawyer will stay up-to-date with these tax laws and help you prepare and update your plan to minimize taxes.

4. Updates

    Kobe Bryant's 7-month-old daughter was left out of his estimated $600 million estate. Although Bryant and his wife had an estate plan in place, the plan failed to name their youngest child, Capri Bryant. The Co-Trustees of the Kobe Bryant Trust filed a Petition to Modify the Trust and add Capri as a beneficiary, and luckily, the petition was granted.

However, the estate planning team made a major error by not updating the plan after Capri's birth or by not including future-born children in the original plan. This mistake cost Kobe's wife Vanessa hefty sums of money to fix, and it also eliminated the trust's biggest benefits by exposing the estate details to the public and keeping his surviving family members out of court.

As Kobe's case shows, estate planning is not a one-and-done deal. Your plan must be updated as your life changes.

Births, deaths, marriages, divorces and incapacity alter a person's life. These life changes also impact the desired income of an estate plan. For example, in many states a divorce automatically invalidates prior Wills and other estate planning documents.

I recommend you review your plan every 3 years and immediately following life events to ensure your family's protection. It's key to have a relationship with an attorney who has a process in place to easily allow for these reviews.

5. Complex Situations

Many people believe they have a simple situation and only need a simple will. However, as the New Jersey example demonstrated, simple can turn out to be unexpectedly complex.

If you are in a blended family, own a business, own real estate out of state, have a disabled family member or a special needs child, or are concerned about asset protection, an estate planning attorney will benefit everyone involved.

For example, when a person has special needs and requires governmental assistance, an inheritance may disqualify them from a critical service. Luckily, specific types of trust can be set up for those with special needs, allowing them to continue to receive benefits and their inheritance. However, setting up a special needs trust is complex and specialized. Working with an experienced estate planning attorney is important to properly protect special needs loved ones.

6. Objectivity

Norm and Paula have three adult children. Their youngest daughter is estranged from them despite all their efforts to reunite. They would like to disinherit her, but they worry about future unintended consequences if they do so.

The Wilsons love their family members, but if something were to happen to them, they'd rather their good friends raise their kids. They worry, though, about how their family will react to this.

Putting an estate plan in place can be an emotional process. Fear, doubt, and guilt can get in the way of making the right decision for you and your loved ones.

Estate planning lawyers can provide objectivity, help you navigate complex family dynamics, and choose the best plan for your family. Discover how easy it is to secure your future, use the Law Mother App to connect with a qualified, trusted estate planning attorney near you, tailored to your unique needs. If you're not quite ready to work with an attorney and prefer some DIY guidance, the app also offers tools and resources to help you take the first steps independently.

TAKING THE FIRST STEPS IN ESTATE PLANNING

Now that you understand the value of a well-thought-out estate plan, it's time to act. It might feel daunting initially, but breaking it into small, manageable steps makes the process much easier. Remember, every step you take helps safeguard your family's future and provides peace of mind. You're not just planning for "what-ifs", you're actively protecting the people and legacy you care about most.

Here's how to get started:

1. Gather Key Information

The initial step in formulating an estate plan is to become organized. Collect all documents that clearly illustrate your financial and personal circumstances.

- List your assets: Include bank accounts, retirement funds, investments, properties, vehicles, and valuable belongings.
- Take stock of your debts: Note any mortgages, loans, or liabilities.
- Review existing policies or documents: Pull records for life insurance, pensions, or other benefits.

Having a clear, updated inventory of your assets and liabilities is critical, not just for you but your loved ones. If something happens to you due to incapacity or passing away, this inventory will clarify and prevent unnecessary stress during an already difficult time. A close friend of mine experienced firsthand the chaos that arises when this step is overlooked. Her father died suddenly without any organization or documentation. It took her *two years* of sifting through his mail, stacks of documents, and various files to piece together what he had and where it was located. Even now, she fears she hasn't found everything, which weighs heavily on her emotions and adds to her uncertainty.

By gathering this information now, you're not just streamlining the process for yourself, you're giving an invaluable gift to those needing to handle your affairs. If you're unsure where to begin, don't stress about perfection. Start by jotting down everything that comes to mind and build from there. This small step can make a world of difference later.

Finding Missing Money with the Department of Unclaimed Property

Each state has a Department of Unclaimed Property, a valuable resource many overlook. Its primary purpose is safeguarding unclaimed money and assets, such as forgotten bank accounts, uncashed checks, insurance payouts, utility deposits, and even safe deposit box contents. If these assets remain unclaimed for a certain period, they are returned to the state for safekeeping.

Finding unclaimed money for yourself or your loved ones can provide peace of mind and even uncover financial resources you didn't realize existed. Here's how to start your search:

- Search Online Databases

  Every state in the U.S. has its own unclaimed property data-base, and many participate in a free national search tool like MissingMoney.com. Begin by entering the name of your loved one, or your own name, to see if any funds are listed. Don't forget to search in every state they've lived or worked in, as unclaimed property is held by the state where it originated.

- Check Federal Resources

  While the states handle most unclaimed property, some funds can only be found through federal agencies. For instance, you can check for missing tax refunds with the IRS or search for unclaimed savings bonds through the Treasury Department.

- Submit a Claim

  If you find unclaimed property, follow the instructions on the website to file a claim. Typically, you must provide documentation proving your identity and connection to the asset, such as a death certificate or proof of the deceased's address.

- Stay Proactive

  Make it a habit to check for unclaimed property periodically. People often misplace or forget about assets over time, so it's worth revisiting these tools every few years.

By taking these steps, you can recover misplaced funds and avoid leaving money behind in the hands of the state. It's a simple yet powerful way to safeguard financial resources for your family, ensuring that no hidden assets slip through the cracks.

2. Prioritize the People Who Matter Most

Next, consider the people you trust to take on important roles in your plan. Start with these key positions:

- Guardian: If you have children or dependents, decide who will care for them if you cannot. This is one of the most critical decisions you'll make, so take time to choose someone whose values align with yours and who can provide stability and love.

- Trustee (Trust) or Executor (Will): This is the individual you'll appoint to ensure your wishes are honored. They should be trustworthy, organized, and capable of handling financial and legal responsibilities.
- Power of Attorney: If you cannot, think about who you trust to make financial and healthcare decisions on your behalf. These individuals play a vital role in protecting your interests while aligning with your values.

Discuss your choices with the people you're considering. Ensure they understand the responsibility and feel comfortable stepping into the role.

3. Define Your Priorities

Before building your plan, ask yourself these questions to guide the process toward the outcomes that matter most to you:

- Who do I want to take care of most? This might include your children, spouse, aging parents, or other loved ones.
- What assets do I want to protect? Consider everything from your family home to savings, heirlooms, and business interests.
- What legacy do I want to leave? Think about how your values and wisdom can live on in the plans you set today.

Clarity on these priorities will help tailor your estate plan to reflect what truly matters to you.

4. Consult a Professional

This step is crucial. An experienced estate planning attorney will help you turn your goals into formal, legally binding documents. While online templates are available, estate planning is rarely a one-size-fits-all process. The guidance of a professional ensures that every detail is taken care of.

An attorney will also help you avoid common pitfalls, like outdated plans or poorly executed documents, and adapt your plan to comply with your state's laws. They can explain your options, answer your questions, and guide you confidently and clearly through the process.

Discover how easy it is to secure your future, use the Law Mother App to connect with a qualified, trusted estate planning attorney near you, tailored to your unique needs. If you're not quite ready to work with an attorney and prefer some DIY guidance, the app also offers tools and resources to help you take the first steps independently.

5. Take It Step by Step—You've Got This

Estate planning doesn't need to be completed all at once. Even taking the first small step, like listing out your priorities or scheduling a consultation, sets you on the right path. You'll gain clarity, confidence, and control over your future with each step.

Remember, estate planning isn't just a legal task, it's a way to say, "I care deeply about my family, and I want to make things easier for them." That guiding intention is your inspiration to move forward, little by little, until your plan is complete.

By acting today, you're creating a future of security, love, and purpose. You're building a legacy, not just of wealth, but of care and intention for the ones who matter most. You're doing this, and you're doing it with heart. Keep going.

7

PROTECT – ASSET PROTECTION FOR WEALTH PRESERVATION

You have worked hard for your assets, and you should not have to fear that courts or creditors will take your assets away before your family can receive the benefits your assets can provide. Asset protection is a crucial part of legal and financial planning. Asset Protection avoids losing your family's assets after you die. Assets include real estate, bank accounts, vehicles, and other property types.

Creditors include frivolous lawsuits, credit card companies, banks, people filing for bankruptcy, and ex-spouses. All these categories of creditors need to be planned for when setting up asset protection strategies.

Asset protection involves structuring a plan to keep funds out of the hands of fraudulent creditors and prevent your assets from being stuck in probate court. When probate courts get involved, money that should go directly to the surviving family is often lost.

Protecting your assets means being intentional about managing them while you are alive and clearly communicating how you want them distributed upon your death.

7 TIPS FOR ASSET PROTECTION & WEALTH PRESERVATION

Asset protection helps families with larger financial assets but can be used by families with a lower net worth. The following are tips for Asset Protection:

1. Avoid a fraudulent conveyance (aka fraudulent transfer in some states)

Asset protection seems like major overkill until you need it. However, if you wait until harm arises, it is too late. The timing of asset protection is important. The first concern is never to defraud your creditors. This type of planning should never start after you've been served with a lawsuit or harm has been done. By that point, it is a *fraudulent* transfer if a transfer of your property is in a manner intended to defraud creditors, which could lead to criminal penalties, civil penalties, and other things that can go wrong.

Claire's Motorcycle Crash

I represented Claire, who was riding on the back of her brother's motorcycle. Claire was with a group of motorcycles going through a green light when a woman named Samantha ran the red light and crashed into them. Claire was seriously injured. Claire lost a limb, and she would have years of expensive surgeries and pain ahead of her. When the police arrived, Claire and the group explained they had the green light. Samantha also told the police she had the green light. The police could not determine who was telling the truth. Two days after the crash, Samantha transferred her $600,000 house to her sister for $10.

In addition to bringing claims against Samantha for the crash, we could bring claims against her for the house transfer; we argued it was a fraudulent conveyance due to the timing of the transfer, just 2 days after the crash at such a low transfer cost. Fraudulent conveyance is a transfer of property made to swindle, hinder, or delay a creditor, or to put such property beyond his or her reach. At trial, we presented the jury with the evidence of Claire's transfer to show consciousness of guilt. The jury ultimately believed our client and awarded her over $4 million.

2. Obtain Proper Insurance & Work with a Trusted Advisor

Daycare Injury

I represented parents whose child was badly injured at a small family-owned daycare. The daycare business had an insurance policy but hadn't read the language carefully. They chose the cheap policy and cut corners, not really understanding the risk they were taking on. Buried in the large policy was an exclusion for common injuries. As a result, the daycare owners had to pay for the child's injuries out of their own pocket - costing them hundreds of thousands of dollars. If they had just paid a few extra dollars a month for extra coverage, they would have had the insurance to cover our client's injuries.

Asset protection planning should never be a substitute for quality insurance. Comprehensive insurance is always the first layer of protection you should have. Consider obtaining property and casualty insurance, liability umbrella policies, commercial insurance, disability insurance, life insurance, professional and malpractice insurance.

Having the right carriers, coverages, and amounts in place will ensure that you have a first line of defense. If you are sued or injured, insurance will step in to help protect the assets you've worked hard to create.

I recommend working with a trusted insurance advisor to get the right coverage. When working with an insurance advisor, speak with them about the type of assets you have and the potential risks. Then go over all the exclusions, the things not covered in the policy. Inquire if you can get coverage or a rider for those exclusions, and what the costs are. The biggest mistake I see is people getting a $1M Umbrella policy and thinking they are fully covered but have a false sense of security. Those exclusions are the holes in the umbrella and there are often affordable riders to fill in those gaps.

If your state has underinsured & uninsured motorist coverage, invest in the highest coverage you can afford. This coverage protects you if your family is hurt in a crash by someone without insurance or the minimum insurance policy (some states only require $15,000 of liability coverage for drivers). For example, I was contacted by a woman who was driving with her family and was T-boned by an uninsured driver. The uninsured driver had no insurance and no assets. This client didn't have uninsured motorist coverage, and the car crash nearly bankrupted her. She was out of work for over a year because of the crash and there was no way to compensate her. She wished she had spent just a few dollars more monthly for uninsured motorist coverage, which would have compensated her and her family for the crash.

3. Start Simple and Utilize Exempt Assets

I received a call from a recent medical school graduate who wanted to set up an offshore asset protection trust (after watching a YouTube video). Offshore Asset protection trusts are costly, expensive to maintain and are not the right solution for everyone. I discovered that the bulk of his assets were in a retirement plan which was already protected from creditors.

The adage of walking before you run is true for asset protection. In most states, assets are protected from creditors by their very nature. Examples include certain types of retirement plans, life insurance, and annuities. In some states, the house you live in is also protected. There was a way to invest and allocate your assets with long-term asset protection.

4. Use of Limited Liability Entities

Creating limited liability companies or other corporate forms to house assets can work to help you protect those assets. If a liability exposure comes out of the business activity in that entity, you can trap those liabilities and protect them from spilling over into your other personal assets.

5. Living Trusts and Domestic asset protection trusts

Living Trusts allow you to protect assets and minimize estate taxes at the death of you or your spouse, and after the second of you passes. If drafted properly and funded correctly, Living Trusts will avoid the probate process. Some states like Wyoming, Nevada, Michigan, and Ohio allow for creation of a domestic asset protection trust ("DAPT").

With a DAPT you can create a trust to hold assets, still have access to those assets, but you can prevent your creditors from being able to reach what's inside the DAPT. These types of trusts are complex and have to be set up properly to avoid any creditor problems.

6. Assemble the Right Team of Advisors

Having Attorneys, CPAs, Financial Advisors and Insurance Brokers specialized in Asset Protection will ensure you are fully protected.

7. Lifetime Asset Protection for Your Children & Grandchildren

Lifetime Asset Protection Trusts, or Dynasty Trusts, protect your children from the above scenarios. Instead of your children receiving their inheritance outright, subjecting the funds to future creditors and divorces, they receive their inheritance in an asset protection trust. You set the terms of the asset protection trust, and the limits. You can put more protection in place, or less, depending on your child's needs.

For example, if your child has an addiction to drugs, alcohol, or gambling now or in the future, you can put protections in place for someone else to be the steward of the money. Additionally, if your child is not good with money, you can appoint a co-trustee to guide their financial decisions.

Charlie's Lost Gift

Charlie's grandfather decided to purchase a house for Charlie and his parents to live in and put the title in Charlie's parents' names. Charlie's grandfather hoped the house would be an asset that Charlie would inherit someday.

Unfortunately, Charlie's mother passed away unexpectedly, and when Charlie's father remarried, he never set up an estate plan. Several years later, Charlie's father also passed away and the house passed to Charlie's stepmother.

Charlie's grandfather was upset. This house was supposed to pass to Charlie, and now it was outside the family with Charlie's estranged stepmother.

Carol's Divorce Loss

Carol inherited $300,000 from her parents when they passed away. At the time Carol was married to an abusive man. Several years later, she finally divorced the man but had to give $150,000 of her parents' hard earned money to her ex-husband.

Two Brothers

Carl and Gary are brothers who each received $500,000 from their parents after they died. Carl invested the money and has over $2 million set aside for his retirement and his grandchild's college fund. In the first year, Gary spent all his share on a new car, travel, and miscellaneous consumer products. He is struggling financially and does not have enough money to retire.

Business Protection

I represented a client who was a bystander at a shooting at a bar. One of the bullets seriously injured him. The insurance policy for the bar would not cover the shooting and so I had to evaluate if the business owner's personal assets would have to pay for this business liability.

We discovered that the bar owner intermingled funds between his business and personal accounts. We also discovered that the bar owner did not properly operate and maintain his business entity, and we had a strong argument to "pierce the corporate veil" and access his personal assets.

If the business owner had properly maintained his business entity, a legal barrier would have prevented us from collecting from his personal and other business assets. A business entity that is properly created, maintained and operated creates a legal barrier between business liability and personal assets.

Small businesses should operate as limited liability entities (an "LLE"). Common forms of LLEs are limited liability companies (LLCs), corporations, and limited partnerships. The available forms of LLEs for small business owners vary by state.

- An LLE provides that the business owners can protect their personal assets from claims brought by the LLE's creditors. This protection is often referred to as the "corporate veil." For example, if a real estate investor purchases a piece of real estate in an LLC, and later there is a fire on the property and the LLC is sued, his personal assets should be protected. There are two ways that a creditor or injured party can get around or "pierce" the corporate veil.

  » If an owner or manager of the LLE is personally responsible for the act that results in a loss or harm to the creditor. For example, if the Owner of a construction company runs a red light and crashes a company vehicle, he is still personally liable for running the red light. He doesn't avoid personal liability even though he was driving for a business purpose on company time.

  » The LLE is not properly operated and maintained by the owner as a business separate from himself or herself.

Proper operation and maintenance of an LLE depends on state-specific laws, and your specific industry's regulations.

The following is a general list of guidelines for properly operating and maintaining an LLE. Working with an experienced Business Attorney to comply with your state's specific laws is prudent.

- Do not commingle personal and business finances. Never pay personal expenses with business funds, or vice versa. To accomplish this, the best practice is to have a separate business bank account for each business and a separate personal bank account.

- Execute and sign business contracts in your representative capacity. For example, sign as Jane Doe, President of Doe Corporation. Do not sign the contract personally as Jane Doe.

- Create and maintain a company record book, including records of all company meetings. For corporations, hold annual meetings for shareholders to elect directors and for directors to select officers.

- Create and maintain company documents. For example, an LLC should maintain an operating agreement. A corporation should maintain articles of incorporation, bylaws, and a stock ownership ledger.
- Regiester all business names with the Secretary of state and file the required annual, biannual or monthly reports in a timely fashion.
- Follow any requirements unique to the state and the industry where your business operates.

Protect What Matters Most

Asset protection is not just for the wealthy, it's for anyone who wants to safeguard what they've worked hard to build. By taking proactive steps to manage and protect your assets, you can ensure they remain secure for your family's future. From understanding the risks, leveraging the right tools like trusts and insurance, and working with trusted advisors, asset protection is a vital part of your financial and legal planning.

Don't leave your wealth to chance, start building your protection plan today. Download the Law Mother App to access professionals in your area, step-by-step videos, and powerful tools to help you create and maintain a strategy that works for you. Secure your future and protect what matters most, because your family's legacy is worth it.

8

PROTECT – TAX MINIMIZATION TO KEEP MORE OF WHAT YOU EARN

The first IRS Audit letter arrived in the middle of the pandemic. My accountant assured me there was no need to panic. "Just send in your bank account statements," he confidently assured me, "and don't worry about the receipts. The IRS won't need them. It'll all be fine."

I wanted to believe him. I was juggling far too much, caring for my newborn, running my legal practice from home, and trying to keep everything in my life afloat as the world around me felt like it was crumbling. For a while, I followed his advice.

Then the second letter arrived, with a more serious tone. The IRS had escalated my case to tax court. My stomach dropped. The reality of the situation was starting to sink in, this wasn't going away, and my accountant wasn't in control.

Desperate and overwhelmed, I called a tax lawyer. Contrary to my accountant's advice, receipts were essential, and more rigor was required.

The next few months were stressful and challenging. Between sleepless nights with a newborn, the demands of my work, and unraveling the mess of my audit, there were moments I thought I wouldn't make it through. The stress was crushing, the stakes high, and only the determination to protect my family's future pushed me forward.

This incredibly painful experience forced me to face a hard truth. I had been too hands-off with my finances, assuming someone else would always have my back. I trusted blindly and didn't take the time to learn the rules myself. What started as one of the most stressful periods of my life became the turning point that changed everything.

By the end of it all, I wasn't just someone who filed taxes; I was someone who understood them. The lessons I learned through that audit gave me clarity, control, and a newfound power over my finances. And now, I'm here to share those lessons with you.

This chapter is about equipping yourself with the tools and knowledge to turn tax management into a financial advantage rather than a source of fear or frustration. Whether you're just starting out, experiencing the highs of a growing income, or managing the complexities of running your own business, you'll learn to keep more of what you've earned and control your future.

Tax planning doesn't have to be intimidating. The right mindset and strategies can empower you to confidently build wealth. Together, we'll turn what feels complex into something you can control.

Regarding your hard-earned money, the power should always rest in your hands.

TAKE THE DRIVER'S SEAT IN YOUR TAXES (WHO WANTS TO BE A BACKSEAT DRIVER IN THEIR FINANCES?)

When it comes to taxes, hands-off is tempting. After all, isn't that why you hired an accountant or bought that fancy tax software? Trust them to take care of it, right? Well, not so fast. Think of taxes as a road trip to financial freedom. It's your money, your future, and ultimately your responsibility. Getting involved doesn't have to be scary. It might even be empowering (and, dare we say, kind of fun?).

Why Being Proactive Matters

Taxes don't reward the passive. Assuming someone else will always "take care of it" is like closing your eyes in a dart game and hoping to hit the bullseye.

Embrace the power to steer your financial future. You don't have to know everything (you're not studying to become an accountant), but understanding how taxes work and what's happening in your own tax return, asking questions, and spotting red flags can help you avoid costly mistakes.

(Oh, and did we mention it's also a great way to keep more of your hard-earned money? Yes!)

The Pitfalls of Blind Trust

Relying blindly on someone else to handle your tax planning is like trusting a stranger with your shopping list, you hope for the best, but you might end up with a bunch of canned peas when you need avocados.

Common mistakes you make when you're hands-off include not providing enough documentation, skipping deductions you didn't know existed, or trusting bad advice from an accountant who may not be as knowledgeable as you thought. Even if you have a great accountant, mistakes can happen. Worse, you might inadvertently hand over some inaccurate information because you didn't know it mattered.

The difference between a **tax preparer** and a **tax strategist** is simple: a preparer records history, while a strategist helps you write it. A tax preparer files your return based on what already happened, but a tax strategist works proactively to structure your income, deductions, and investments in a way that legally minimizes your tax burden, so you keep more of what you earn.

Take it from me, as someone who once trusted entirely the wrong advice from "the expert," there's too much at stake to stay passive.

How to Start Taking Control (Yes, You Can Totally Do This)

Taking control of your taxes doesn't have to mean long hours drowning in paperwork and complex calculations. It's about developing good habits and getting a lay of the land. Here are three simple steps to help you start:

1. **Track Everything**

   Begin by keeping tabs on your income, expenses, and any big financial events. Did you sell a house this year? Maybe you started freelancing on the side? Every transaction matters, and having a record makes filing (and audits!) way less stressful.

2. **Learn Tax Basics**

   You don't need to be a tax wizard, but understanding a few basics will help you make sense of your own numbers. Start with things like knowing how tax brackets work or what tax credits and deductions are available to you. Not sure where to begin? Check out IRS.gov (seriously, their site is surprisingly helpful), or find some beginner-friendly resources online.

3. Make Documentation Your Friend

This is possibly the least glamorous part of taxes but easily one of the most important. Get in the habit of organizing and storing all your tax-related documents. Physical files work fine, but a digital setup like folders on Google Drive can save a ton of space, and subdue panic when you suddenly need something.

The rule? If you think you *might* need it, save it. Can you have too many receipts? Maybe, but it is better than *not enough* if the IRS comes knocking.

YOUR MONEY, YOUR RULES

Ultimately, taking ownership of your taxes means saying, "This is my money, I'm going to protect it." Not only does it empower you to avoid the stress of mistakes or audits, but it also helps you use the system to your advantage. That's the real goal here, to turn taxes from something dreaded into part of building wealth.

Tax Basics – Lay the Foundation
(How to Stop Tax Talk from Sounding Like Gibberish)

Taxes have a bad reputation. They're often seen as confusing, overwhelming, and maybe even something to avoid until absolutely necessary (hello, last-minute filing on April 14th).

Understanding the basics of how taxes work is like learning the rules of a game. Once you know how to play, it's easier to win.

So, grab your favorite beverage, and let's break down the fundamentals. By the time we're done here, you'll feel a lot more confident about navigating the world of taxes, and keeping more of your money in the process.

How Income Is Taxed

First, you're not taxed on every single dollar you earn equally. The U.S. tax system is progressive, which means your income gets taxed in chunks, starting with the lowest rate and moving progressively to higher rates as you earn more.

Here's an example: Imagine there are three tax brackets for simplicity's sake, 10%, 20%, and 30%. If you made $50,000 in a year, your income could be split across those brackets. The first $10,000 might be taxed at 10%, the next $20,000 at 20%, and the last $20,000 at 30%. This ensures that people pay higher rates only on the portion of income into those higher brackets.

Marginal vs. Effective Tax Rates

Now, here's where people sometimes get tripped up.

Your **marginal tax rate** is the tax rate on the *last* dollar you earned, it's that top bracket you've reached. Your **effective tax rate** is the average rate you pay on your total income after accounting for all the brackets.

For example, in our $50,000 scenario, while your marginal rate might be 30%, your effective rate could be closer to 20% because a lot of your income was taxed at lower rates. Sounds a little better now, doesn't it?

Understanding this distinction can help you better plan your finances and take advantage of strategies to lower your taxable income, which leads us to…

Tax-Advantaged Accounts – Your Best Friends

One of the smartest ways to reduce your taxable income and plan for the future is to use tax-advantaged accounts. These accounts are like secret weapons that help you save for retirement or big life expenses *while* keeping more of your money out of Uncle Sam's hands (legally, of course).

Here's a quick rundown of the heavy hitters and what they can do for you:

- 401(k): Offered by many employers, this retirement account lets you contribute pre-tax dollars, lowering your taxable income today. Your money grows tax-deferred, and you'll pay taxes only when you withdraw it in retirement. Bonus points if your employer matches your contributions! That's free money!

- Roth IRA: You contribute after-tax dollars, and your money grows tax-free. When you withdraw it in retirement, you owe zero taxes on it. Cha-ching!
- Traditional IRA: This is similar to a 401(k), but it's not tied to an employer. Contributions are usually tax-deductible, and your money grows tax-deferred, you are taxed when you eventually withdraw the money, possibly in a lower tax bracket at retirement.
- SEP IRA: Perfect for self-employed folks or small business owners, this allows you to save for retirement with higher contribution limits than a traditional IRA, and you can deduct those contributions from your taxable income.

These accounts allow you to save while reducing your taxable income now or avoiding taxes later. Either way, it's a win for your wallet.

Turning Basics into Big Wins

By mastering these building blocks, you can make smarter financial decisions, keep more of your income, and tax-plan like a pro. It doesn't take a tax degree, just a willingness to learn, ask questions, and take charge of your own finances.

Pretty soon, you'll realize that taxes aren't the confusing beast they appear to be. They're just another tool you can use to your advantage. Isn't that what financial freedom is all about?

Estate Tax Minimization

When someone passes away, their property and money, called their "estate", can be taxed before it goes to their family or loved ones. The IRS explains this as a tax on money and property you own at death that you want to pass on. This includes things like houses, cash, stocks, businesses, and cars.

To determine how much is taxed, the value of everything is added up to get the gross estate. After that, certain costs are taken away, like debts, funeral costs, and any money left to a spouse or charity. What's left is called your taxable estate.

For 2025, a person can pass on up to $13.99 million without paying federal estate taxes. If you're married, that doubles to $27.98 million for both of you. This is called the estate tax exemption. If your taxable estate is higher than these amounts, the tax rate is 40%.

You can also give money as a gift while you're alive to avoid taxes later. For 2025, you can give up to $19,000 per person yearly (or $38,000 if you're married).

What About State Estate and Inheritance Taxes?

Some states also have their own estate or inheritance taxes, which are extra taxes on the estate.

Here's a simple breakdown for 2025:

Connecticut: Estate tax on estates over $13,990,000 (12% rate).

District of Columbia: Estate tax on estates over $4,873,200 (16% rate).

Hawaii: Estate tax on estates over $5,490,000 (20% rate).

Illinois: Estate tax on estates over $4,000,000 (up to 16% rate).

Iowa: Inheritance tax eliminated as of January 1, 2025.

Kentucky: Inheritance tax applies to non-immediate family ($500–$1,000 exemption).

Maine: Estate tax on estates over $7,000,000 (up to 12% rate).

Maryland: Estate tax on estates over $5,000,000 (16% rate); inheritance tax up to 10%.

Massachusetts: Estate tax on estates over $2,000,000 (up to 16% rate).

Minnesota: Estate tax on estates over $3,000,000 (up to 16% rate).

Nebraska: Inheritance tax with exemptions of $100,000 (close relatives) and $25,000–$40,000 (others); rates range from 1% to 15%.

New Jersey: Inheritance tax applies to non-immediate family ($25,000 exemption).

New York: Estate tax on estates over $7,160,000 (up to 16% rate, with a cliff tax for estates exceeding 105% of the exemption).

Oregon: Estate tax on estates over $1,000,000 (up to 16% rate).

Pennsylvania: Inheritance tax rates: 0% (spouse/minor children), 4.5% (adult children/lineal relatives), 12% (siblings), 15% (others).

Rhode Island: Estate tax on estates over $1,802,431 (adjusted annually for inflation).

Vermont: Estate tax on estates over $5,000,000 (16% rate).

Washington: Estate tax on estates over $2,193,000 (up to 20% rate).

How to Reduce or Avoid Estate Taxes

There are smart ways to protect your money and property from high taxes when you pass away. These include:

1. Gifting Early—Give money or property to your family while you're still alive within the gift tax limits.
2. Using Trusts—Special setups like Life Insurance Trusts or Family Trusts can protect your assets and reduce taxes.
3. Donating to Charity—Leaving money or property to a charity can lower the taxable amount of your estate.
4. Planning with Experts—Working with estate planners, lawyers, or tax professionals can make sure everything is done right.

Estate tax laws can change, so it's important to stay updated. With the right plan, you can save your loved ones from paying too much and ensure your money and property go where you want.

Strategies for Different Incomes

When it comes to taxes, one size definitely does not fit all. Your income level plays a huge role in the strategies that will work best for you. But no matter where you fall on the income spectrum, there are ways to reduce your tax burden and make the system work in your favor.

Whether you're just getting by, comfortably cruising, or hitting the high-earner stratosphere, we've got tailored strategies to help you save more and stress less.

For Low-Income Earners (Where Every Dollar Counts)

If you're in a lower income bracket, taxes might feel less like something to plan for and more like something to worry about. Fortunately, you might actually qualify for benefits and breaks that could leave more money in your pocket.

- Maximize Tax Credits

  Tax credits are like free money, they reduce your tax bill dollar-for-dollar. One biggie to know about is the Earned Income Tax Credit (EITC). It's designed for low- to moderate-income workers and can put thousands of dollars back in your pocket if you qualify. Another important one? The Child Tax Credit if you have kids. These credits can significantly reduce or even eliminate the taxes you owe.

- Don't Forget the Saver's Credit

  Did you know you can get a tax credit for saving for retirement? If you're contributing to a retirement account like a 401(k) or IRA and your income meets certain thresholds, you might qualify for the Saver's Credit, reducing your tax bill and setting you up for the future. Talk about a Win-Win!

- File Your Taxes, Even If You Don't Think You Need To

  Even if your income is low enough that you're not required to file taxes, doing so is essential if you want to claim refunds or credits you're eligible for. Skipping this step could mean missing out on free cash that's rightfully yours.

For Middle-Income Earners (The Power of Planning)

A lot of middle-income earners feel stuck, they make too much to qualify for certain credits but not enough to take advantage of the strategies we'll cover for high-earners. Don't worry, there are plenty of ways to lower your tax bill and stay on top of your finances.

- Leverage Tax-Advantaged Accounts

  Make the most of retirement accounts like a 401(k), Traditional IRA, or Roth IRA. Contributing to these accounts not only sets you up for retirement but can also reduce your taxable income now. For instance, 401(k) contributions are made with pre-tax dollars, lowering your income for the year (and potentially dropping you into a lower tax bracket so you'll pay less in taxes).

- Get Smart About Deductions

  Are you claiming every deduction you can? If you own a home, mortgage interest and property taxes could mean big savings. Deductions like medical expenses, student loan interest, and even education-related costs can add up. If you're self-employed, don't forget deductions for a home office, equipment, or business travel.

- Consider an HSA or FSA

  Health savings accounts (HSAs) and flexible spending accounts (FSAs) are great tools for middle-income earners. They allow you to set aside pre-tax dollars for healthcare expenses, meaning you save on taxes while covering medical needs. Bonus with HSAs: unused funds roll over year after year, making them a double-duty savings account.

For High-Income Earners (Bring on the Advanced Moves)

Once you start earning more, taxes begin to feel like an uphill battle. But with higher income comes more opportunities for savvy tax strategies. Yes, the IRS has its eye on you, but that doesn't mean you can't put your money to work smartly.

- Charitable Giving

  Feeling generous? High-income earners can get a solid tax break by donating to qualified charities. Contributions of cash, appreciated stock, or even property can help reduce your tax bill while making a difference. Plus, tactics like donor-advised funds makes charitable giving even more tax-efficient.

- Tax-Loss Harvesting

  This strategy is a golden goose for high-income investors. You can offset gains from your winners by selling investments that have lost value. It's a way to reduce your taxable income and hold onto more of your profits. It's like finding the silver lining in a market downturn.

- Use Trusts to Your Advantage

  Trusts are not just for the super-wealthy; they're a useful way to manage wealth and distribute assets in a tax-optimized manner. Options like revocable living trusts, charitable trusts, or grantor-retained annuity trusts (GRATs) can help reduce estate taxes and secure your financial legacy for loved ones.

- Max Out Deferred Compensation Plans

  If your employer offers deferred compensation plans, take advantage of them. These allow you to delay accessing some of your income until retirement, potentially reducing your current taxable income and bumping that money into a lower tax bracket in the future.

- Explore Alternative Investments

  High-income earners can consider alternative investments like real estate, private equity, or hedge funds. Not only can these diversify your portfolio and potentially yield higher returns, but they may also come with unique tax advantages, such as depreciation deductions or opportunity zone investments.

The Golden Rule of Income-Based Tax Strategies

Regardless of your income level, planning, documenting, and being proactive is key to winning the tax game. Know what's available to you, whether it's a credit, deduction, or investment strategy, and ensure you're taking full advantage.

Taxes may feel like a chore, but when you align your financial habits with your income level and long-term goals, they transform into a roadmap to keeping and growing more of your money.

Because, in the end, it's not just about what you earn, it's about what you keep.

Business Owners and Entrepreneurs – Play to Your Strengths

Being a business owner or entrepreneur is an adventure, you get to set your goals, work on your terms, and take charge of your future.

It also means your taxes are a whole different ball game. Tax planning isn't just a side note for you; it's a critical part of your overall business strategy. With the right approach, you can turn taxes from a headache into an opportunity to boost your bottom line.

Why Tax Planning for Business Owners Is Fundamentally Different

When running a business, your tax situation isn't simple, like filling in a W-2 and calling it a day. Your income may fluctuate from year to year. You've got expenses, investments, and employees (possibly even yourself!).

Flexibility is your superpower, and when you lean into the unique advantages available to business owners, you can keep more of your hard-earned money.

Maximize Deductions with Smart Expense Categorization

The secret to lowering your tax bill lies in how you track and categorize your expenses. Every penny you spend on your business can potentially reduce your taxable income—IF it's documented properly.

- Track Every Expense

  Keep a detailed record of every business-related expense, from office supplies to your internet bill. Tools like bookkeeping software or a financial app can help you stay organized and avoid searching through scattered paper receipts.

- Understand What's Deductible

  Deductions include marketing costs, business travel, professional services (like hiring an accountant), and meals with clients (50% of the cost). Think beyond the obvious, your home office, phone bills, and even a percentage of your utilities might qualify. Learn the rules so you don't leave money on the table.

Tax-Minimization Strategies You Need

Want to keep more money in your pocket? It's all about using the tools available to you. Here are some strategies successful business owners swear by:

- Depreciation Matters

  If you've purchased equipment, vehicles, or office space for your business, you can deduct their value over time through depreciation. Bonus depreciation is a game-changer, it allows you to deduct a large portion (sometimes all) of an asset's cost upfront. For big-ticket items, this can significantly reduce your tax bill in the year you purchase them.

- Employ Family Members!

  Hiring family members (your spouse or teenage child) to work for your business keeps the operation close-knit and reduces your taxable income. Wages paid to family members become deductible business expenses, and if they fall into a lower tax bracket, it's a win-win for your family members. Just make sure the work and wages are properly documented.

  Pro Tip: Curious about hiring your kids? Check out the "Kids on Payroll" course in the Law Mother app for step-by-step guidance on how to do it correctly. You'll save on taxes and you'll also teach your kids valuable financial lessons!

- Set Up a Tax-Advantaged Retirement Plan

  Business owners have some of the best options when it comes to retirement planning. Set up a Solo 401(k) if you're self-employed or a SEP IRA for a simple yet effective way to save for retirement while lowering taxes. These plans let you contribute much more than a traditional IRA, giving you a tax break now and a nest egg for your future.

- Use the Augusta Rule

  The Augusta Rule lets you rent out your personal home to your business for up to 14 days per year without paying taxes on the income. The rental payment is deductible as a business expense, but you don't get taxed on it (if it's priced fairly based on market rates). This is a smart way for business owners to use their personal property to benefit their business while enjoying a tax-free boost.

- Take Advantage of the Home Office Deduction

  You can claim the home office deduction if you work from home or operate part of your business there. This allows you to deduct expenses like a portion of your rent or mortgage, utilities, internet, and even home insurance. The key is that the space must be used *exclusively* for business. Even a small home office can mean significant savings on your taxes.

Consider Alternative Investments

Thinking outside the box can succeed big time regarding tax advantages. Certain investments not only grow your wealth but also provide significant tax benefits.

- Real Estate Is a Gold Mine

  Owning commercial or residential properties leads to deductions for mortgage interest, property taxes, and operating expenses. Plus, you can take advantage of *depreciation*, which allows you to deduct the cost of the property's wear and tear over time, even if property values are rising. The short term rental tax loophole is also a powerful strategy to investigate.

- Bonus Depreciation for Real Estate

  Recent tax rules allow you to combine real estate investments with bonus depreciation. For example, if you purchase assets like furniture, fixtures, or certain building improvements for your property, you could deduct those costs much faster than before.

- Investing in Solar Energy

  Going green doesn't just benefit the planet, it can also do wonders for your taxes. Investing in solar energy systems for your business may qualify for the federal Investment Tax Credit (ITC), which currently allows you to deduct up to 50% of the cost of your solar installation. Solar investments often qualify for accelerated depreciation under the Modified Accelerated Cost Recovery System (MACRS), letting you deduct a significant portion of your investment in the first few years. This is a smart tax move and can lower your energy bills and boost your business's eco-friendly image.

These strategies are all about keeping more of what you earn, but they require proper documentation and planning. By working with a CPA or tax professional, you can make sure you're taking full advantage of what the tax code offers.

Keeping It All Together

Tax planning is only effective if you stay organized. Poor record-keeping is one of the most common pitfalls for small business owners, and it can lead to missed opportunities and unwanted headaches if the IRS comes knocking.

- Leverage Professional Help

  Bring a tax pro into your corner, someone who understands the unique challenges of business taxes and can help you uncover strategies you might never think about. Consider it an investment in your business, because every deduction and credit they uncover boosts your financial health.

If you're looking for a tax pro, we'll cover additional resources in the final chapter and on the *Law Mother app* to help you find the right fit.

Taxes can feel like an enormous responsibility when managing a business, but they don't have to drain your time or energy. With a proactive approach, you'll uncover opportunities to grow, save, and maximize what's yours. Use these strategies to play to your strengths and create a tax plan that works as hard as you do.

Wrap-Up: Harnessing the Power of Strong Tax Habits

Taxes may never be your favorite topic, but building strong tax habits can be among the most empowering things for your financial future. It's not just about avoiding mistakes or lowering your tax bill (although both are great perks!). It's about creating stability, boosting your confidence, and feeling in control of your money. When you understand your taxes, you're no longer at their mercy.

A Painful Lesson Turned into Empowerment

When I look back at my own tax journey, I'll admit I've made mistakes. There was one particularly painful audit that felt overwhelming at the time. The IRS flagged my return, and while sifting through the paperwork, I realized I had overlooked some critical details in my tax preparation. After some time, research, and back-and-forth negotiations, we settled for a reasonable amount. It wasn't fun but wasn't the end of the world. It was the wake-up call I needed.

It drove me to better understand my taxes, how they work, where I went wrong, and what I could do better. I hired a more qualified tax strategist. Not only has this person helped me avoid further mistakes, but they've also uncovered strategies that save me thousands of dollars each year. What started as a moment of dread became a turning point that put me in the driver's seat of my financial future.

Take Ownership and Keep What You Earn

You have more control over your taxes than you might realize. You can hold onto more of your hard-earned money by owning your financial decisions and adopting a strategic approach. Strong tax habits aren't reserved for the wealthy, they're for anyone who wants to create financial freedom and build long-term stability.

The key is to stop seeing taxes as a messy pile of forms and numbers and start viewing them as a powerful tool. Every deduction, credit, and proactive plan is an opportunity to build security and grow wealth.

Action Steps to Build Strong Tax Habits

Here's how to get started on your path to tax confidence and financial freedom.

1. **Stay Organized Year-Round**

   Keep detailed records of your income, expenses, and investments. Use tools (like a bookkeeping app) to avoid last-minute stress.

2. **Hire Professional Help When Needed**

   Partner with a qualified tax strategist or CPA who understands your unique needs, whether you're an entrepreneur, a freelancer, or a salaried worker.

3. **Learn the Basics of Tax Law**

   You don't have to become an expert, but understanding key deductions, credits, and tax planning rules can save you money and stress.

4. **Plan Ahead**

   Don't wait until April rolls around, schedule regular tax check-ins to ensure you're on track and avoid surprises.

5. **Leverage Tax-Advantaged Accounts**

   Maximize tools like retirement accounts (401(k), IRA, etc.) and health savings accounts (HSA) to reduce taxable income.

6. **Invest Strategically**

   Consider tax-smart investments like real estate, solar energy, or retirement plans that align with your financial goals while lowering your tax burden.

7. **Reflect and Learn from Mistakes**

   Every oversight or misstep is a chance to grow. Use these moments to refine your strategy and make smarter decisions in the future.

8. **Tap Into Resources**

   Explore tools like the Law Mother app or reach out to financial professionals to guide you every step of the way.

Taxes don't have to feel like a mystery or a burden. By taking small, consistent steps toward stronger habits and informed decisions, you'll save money and gain peace of mind. Remember, you've worked hard for your money. It's time to make sure more of it stays with you.

Now act, stay curious, and build a secure and prosperous future. You've got this!

9

LIVE YOUR WEALTHY EVER AFTER

For years, I believed earning more money was the key to financial security. I worked tirelessly, landed a high-paying job as a litigator, and eventually built my own law firm. Yet, instead of feeling secure, I was constantly racing to stay ahead. Between payroll, taxes, and unexpected expenses, my bank account felt more like a revolving door than a financial fortress. The stress never truly disappeared, it just changed forms.

Then, I uncovered something that changed everything. More importantly, I acted on it.

I realized that the wealthiest families, the billionaires, the iconic dynasties like the Rockefellers, and the financially free individuals I worked with, weren't just lucky. They didn't succeed through random victories or one-time windfalls.

They followed a clear, repeatable system.

They didn't just earn money. They didn't just invest. And they didn't just try to keep what they had. They cycled through three core wealth-building actions, over and over again, ensuring their financial security didn't just last for their lifetime but for generations.

I call these The 3 Wealth Accelerators

GROW:

Establish a solid foundation by transforming your money mindset, organizing your finances, and expanding your income streams. You're no longer just earning money, you're intentionally directing it toward your goals.

MULTIPLY:

Make your money work for you through strategic investing, passive income, and sustainable wealth-building habits. You're shifting from relying solely on your effort to letting your money grow.

PROTECT:

Safeguard your wealth to ensure it lasts. Minimize taxes, secure your assets, and create a robust financial plan to preserve your legacy for generations.

This is the cycle of true, lasting wealth, a process the wealthiest families repeat, refine, and strengthen over time. They don't just accumulate money; they consistently grow, multiply, and protect it for the long term.

But here's the problem, most people are never taught this.

Why I Wrote This Book

One night at 3 AM, while breastfeeding my second child, I recorded a rough video sharing these lessons. The lighting was terrible. The sound was worse. But it didn't matter, *it got 6 million views.* So I made another. And another. Within months, I had over a million followers. Then, The Drew Barrymore Show called.

But even with all the videos, the messages kept coming in:

"I don't know where to start."
"I wish someone would just give me a roadmap."
"Why didn't anyone teach me this sooner?"

I wrote *Wealthy Ever After* to give you that roadmap.

This book isn't just about learning what the wealthy do, it's about applying it in your own life. That's why I created the Law Mother app as well, to provide the tools, structure, and expert connections necessary to turn knowledge into action.

Because financial success isn't just about knowing what to do.

It's about doing it.

Now, you have access to the same repeatable system that has helped the wealthiest families protect and grow their wealth for generations.

THIS IS YOUR TURNING POINT

I saw this pattern in my clients' experiences and my journey. Like many others, I once believed that working harder, earning more, or investing smarter would eliminate financial stress. But more money doesn't solve the problem without a system, it just makes it bigger.

I wrote *Wealthy Ever After*, to give you the blueprint to create lasting financial freedom.

NOW, IT'S YOUR TURN

Wealth isn't just something you acquire, it's something you maintain, expand, and secure over time. You are now equipped with the knowledge and strategies to create your *Wealthy Ever After*.

What You'll Learn in This Chapter

You've learned how to Grow, Multiply, and Protect your wealth at this stage. Now, it's time to apply those principles to your everyday life with three essential steps:

1. Creating an Intentional Spending Plan: This isn't about restriction; it's about aligning your spending with your values and long-term goals. True financial freedom comes from knowing where your money is going and ensuring it's working for you.
2. Choosing the Right Advisors: Wealthy people don't build and protect their assets alone. They surround themselves with the

right professionals, financial planners, tax strategists, and legal experts, to help them make informed decisions.

3. Execute: Knowledge alone won't change your financial future, execution will. This chapter will guide you through real, actionable steps to ensure you're not just absorbing information but putting it into practice. The key to lasting wealth is not just learning the cycle but committing to repeating it.

Step-by-Step Guide to Crafting Your Intentional Spending Plan

Creating a spending plan is like designing a roadmap to your financial success. By aligning your money with your values and goals, you gain a sense of purpose and control over your finances. This guide builds directly on the *Wealthy Vision* and *Stairway to Wealthy* framework introduced in Chapter 2, showing you how to use it as the foundation to craft your personalized spending plan and take actionable steps toward your wealth vision.

In Chapter 2, we laid the groundwork by helping you define your financial priorities and establish a clear vision for success. This chapter introduced the *Stairway to Wealthy*, a powerful 8-step framework designed to guide you through the building blocks of saving, eliminating debt, and creating long-term financial security. These steps structure your goals and provide the clarity you need to take control of your finances.

Revisiting the 8 Steps of the Stairway to Wealthy

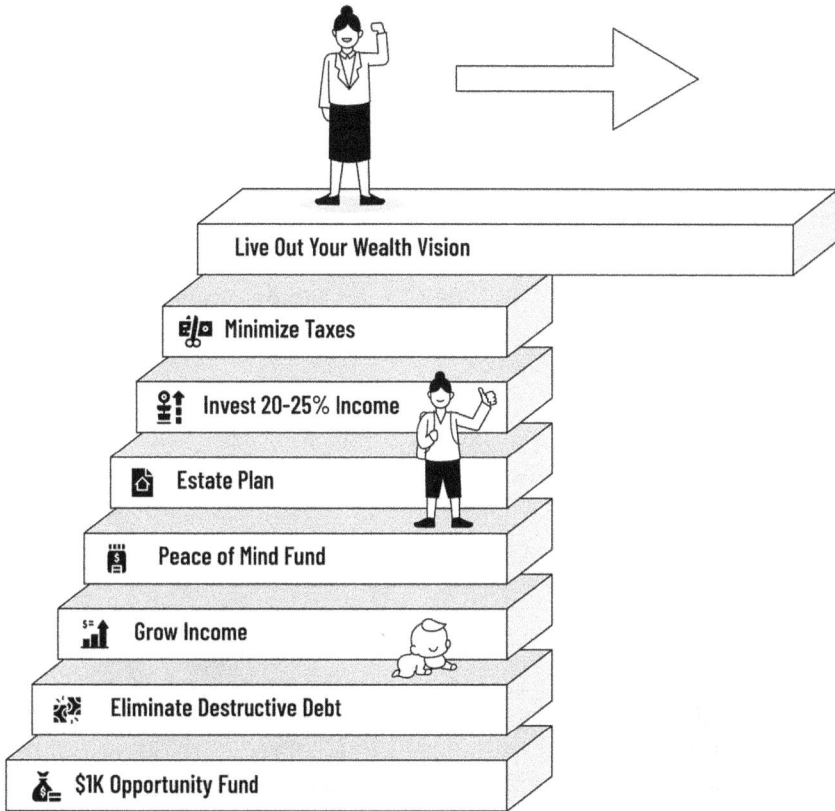

Live Out Your Wealth Vision

Minimize Taxes

Invest 20-25% Income

Estate Plan

Peace of Mind Fund

Grow Income

Eliminate Destructive Debt

$1K Opportunity Fund

The Wealth Ladder is your blueprint for achieving financial stability and growth. Here's a refresher on its nine steps, each designed to build on the progress of the last:

1. Save $1,000 in an Opportunity Fund: Your first step to financial peace is creating a small safety net, stored in a high-yield savings account.
2. Eliminate Destructive Debt (excluding mortgage): Take control of high-interest credit card debt to stop it from draining your potential.
3. Grow Your Income: Focus on expanding your earning potential.
4. Set up a Peace of Mind Fund: Build on your savings by amassing three to six months of essential expenses in a high-yield savings account.

5. Set up Your Estate Plan: Ensure your loved ones are protected, obtain life insurance if necessary.

6. Invest 20-25% of Income: Commit to steady investment in vehicles like retirement plans, brokerage accounts, or real estate for long-term growth.

7. Minimize Taxes: Optimize your strategy through tax-efficient investing, contributions to retirement accounts, and understanding write-offs.

8. Repeat, Living Your Wealth Vision: Continue refining and optimizing your plan while living the financially empowered life you've built.

Each step on the Wealth Ladder brings you closer to financial freedom. Integrating it into your spending plan will create a strategic path for achieving your goals, whether paying off debt, saving for the future, or investing in wealth-building opportunities.

Using the Stairway to Wealthy to Identify Your First Financial Goal

The Stairway to Wealthy, introduced in Chapter 2, assists you in prioritizing your financial goals; however, your starting point depends on your progress. Each step builds on the one before, so determining your starting point requires evaluating what you have already accomplished.

For example, if you don't have any savings yet, your priority is building an *Opportunity Fund* by saving $1,000 in a high-yield savings account. If you've already saved $1,000, move on to focusing on debt repayment.

Exploring Spending Plan Levels

A successful financial beginner starts with understanding your situation and creating a plan that evolves alongside you. The four spending plan levels below correspond with the Stairway to Wealthy framework and percentages, enabling you to make the most of your money. Whether you're just starting or looking to maximize wealth-building opportunities, there's a plan suited to you.

Plan Level	Category	Percentage
Starter	Needs	70%
	Wants	20%
	Savings & Investing	10%
Intermediate	Needs	50%
	Wants	30%
	Savings & Investing	20%
Advanced	Needs	30%
	Wants	20%
	Savings & Investing	50%
Expert	Needs	10%
	Wants	10%
	Savings & Investing	80%

Starter Level Spending Plan

The Starter level is perfect for breaking free from the cycle of living paycheck to paycheck. At this stage, you focus on regaining control, beginning to save, and developing financial confidence.

Spending Breakdown:

- Needs: 70%
- Wants: 20%
- Savings and Investing: 10%

Actionable Strategies:

- *Focus on Basic Needs:* Allocate most of your income to essentials, such as rent, groceries, and transportation. Manage your expenses carefully to avoid overspending.
- *Start Tracking Expenses:* Develop the habit of writing down where your money is going. This awareness will set the stage for intentional financial decisions. Alternatively, automate this step through a financial app.
- *Establish an Opportunity Fund:* Although savings might not be a priority, any extra resources should be directed towards Step 1 on the Stairway to Wealthy (saving $1,000 in an Opportunity Fund). Even modest contributions can build momentum.
- *Mindful Wants:* With 20% allocated to wants, avoid splurging and find low-cost ways to enjoy life while maintaining discipline.

This is the foundation of your spending plan. Use this phase to identify key values and build confidence in managing your finances.

Intermediate Level Spending Plan

At the Intermediate level, you're becoming more aware of your spending, living within your means, and concentrating on boosting your income and establishing your financial safety net.

Spending Breakdown:

- Needs: 50%
- Wants: 30%
- Savings and Investing: 20%+

Actionable Strategies:

- *Reduce Necessary Costs:* Find ways to lower fixed expenses such as housing or utilities. With fewer resources allocated to needs, you'll create more room for wealth-building.
- *Expand Your Peace of Mind Fund:* Save three to six months of expenses in a high-yield savings account. This Peace of Mind Fund will safeguard you during financial setbacks.

- *Learn and Grow:* Explore opportunities to grow income by developing new skills or pursue one of the Five income streams. You're actively building momentum at this stage, integrating the Stairway to Wealthy's principles to create a stable financial base.

Advanced Level Spending Plan

The advanced level focuses on building wealth through investments and strategic planning. You have established financial security and are now directing resources toward long-term growth.

Spending Breakdown:

- Needs: 30%
- Wants: 20%
- Savings and Investing: 50%+

Actionable Strategies:

- *Invest Assertively:* With more than half of your income directed towards savings and investments, allocate funds into retirement accounts, index funds, and real estate opportunities. Fully fund retirement accounts and consider diversified portfolios for greater returns.
- *Tax Strategies:* Minimize taxes by contributing to tax-advantaged accounts like a 401(k) or IRA, and understand advanced tax strategies
- *Build Your Legacy:* Solidify your estate plan and protect your loved ones with life insurance.
- *Reassess "Wants":* Prioritize discretionary spending that aligns with hobbies, self-care, or family time, but control it to maximize savings.

At this level, wealth building is no longer a dream but a reality. Intentional choices keep you aligned with lasting financial freedom.

Expert Level Spending Plan

The Expert level is for those who've mastered financial discipline and are focused on sustained growth, philanthropy, and optimizing every part of their plan.

Spending Breakdown:

- Needs: 10%
- Wants: 10%
- Savings and Investing: 80%+

Actionable Strategies:

- *Focus on Giving:* With needs and wants streamlined, use your financial power to support your passions and impact communities. This could include philanthropy, mentoring, or funding social causes.
- *Perfect Your Plan:* Periodically reassess your estate plan, tax strategies, and longer-term investment goals. Sheer proactivity ensures financial success remains aligned with your vision.
- *Enjoy Freedom:* With stability established, use this phase to focus on personal enjoyment and achieve meaningful experiences on your terms.

This is the pinnacle of financial planning. You've achieved mastery, and now, your resource allocation reflects your values and lasting financial empowerment.

CREATING YOUR ADVISORY TEAM

Achieving financial freedom is a collaborative effort. Surrounding yourself with the right experts and supporters can make all the difference in your wealth-building journey. Your advisory team isn't merely a group of professionals; it's a powerhouse of knowledge, guidance, and encouragement tailored to your unique needs and goals.

An advisory team is your network of specialists and supporters who collaborate with you to provide expertise, hold you accountable, and keep you motivated. Each member is vital in ensuring you make informed decisions and maintain steady progress toward your financial dreams.

Navigating your finances on your own can feel overwhelming at times. But with a trusted team in your corner, you gain clarity, confidence, and the tools to make smarter, faster decisions. The combined support of your advisory team empowers you to overcome challenges and capitalize on opportunities you might not have seen otherwise.

Who should be on your team?

To build a comprehensive advisory team, focus on assembling the following key experts and supporters at the right stage in your wealth building journey. Their combined skills and insights will provide the balanced support you need as you move through each stage of the Stairway to Wealthy:

1. Financial Advisor: A financial advisor helps you create a comprehensive financial plan tailored to your long-term goals. While the Law Mother App and book offer an excellent starting point for building your plan independently, there may be times when additional professional support is beneficial. A skilled financial advisor can enhance your efforts if you feel stuck, uncertain, or as your assets grow. They provide deeper insights into managing investments, retirement planning, and risk management when it matters most.

2. Tax Strategist: This can be a CPA or a tax attorney who specializes in minimizing your tax obligations. They will assist you in understanding tax-efficient investing, taking advantage of deductions, and developing strategies to preserve more wealth. This is especially crucial if you are a business owner or a high earner.

3. Estate Planning Lawyer: To protect your assets and secure your family's future, an estate planning lawyer ensures a comprehensive plan for distributing wealth.

4. Business Lawyer: If you're a business owner, a lawyer specializing in business law can safeguard your company's legal interests, guide contracts, and help structure your business for optimal profitability and legal safety.

5. Mindset/Life Coach: A mindset or life coach focuses on your mindset, habits, and emotional relationship with money and other priorities in your life. They are an ongoing source of encouragement and support, helping you overcome mental roadblocks that could slow your progress.

Each specialist brings something unique, but they all share one critical requirement: alignment with your vision for financial freedom. When creating your team, prioritize professionals who understand your values and support your long-term aspirations.

Using the Law Mother App

Building this team may seem daunting, but the Law Mother App simplifies the process. The app connects you directly with skilled financial advisors, tax strategists, estate and business lawyers, and financial coaches, all in one platform. Whether you're just starting or fine-tuning your plans, you'll find the support and expertise you need right at your fingertips.

The app also provides access to a community of like-minded individuals with similar financial goals. These connections help keep you motivated while fostering a sense of accountability and shared purpose.

Your Path to Success

You don't need to have all the answers or navigate this journey alone. The right advisory team empowers you to make informed decisions, avoid costly mistakes, and expedite your goals. By leveraging tools like the Law Mother App, you can bring these skilled professionals together and create the support system you deserve.

Begin assembling your team today, confident that with the right experts, you'll possess everything necessary to achieve financial success and build the life you envisioned. With trusted guidance, each step forward becomes easier, bringing your freedom closer than you realize.

Staying Committed with Community Support

The road to financial freedom is filled with ups and downs. While having a strong plan and an expert team is crucial, another often-overlooked force is the power of community. Being part of a supportive group can make the difference between giving up when challenges arise and pushing through to achieve your goals. When you surround yourself with people who share your aspirations, everything transforms. A community fosters an environment where motivation thrives, and setbacks don't seem insurmountable. Accountability serves as a powerful driver of progress. Suddenly, your financial planning is no longer a solitary task but a supportive group effort where victories, lessons, and even challenges are shared.

Communities inspire action in ways that self-discipline alone cannot. Witnessing others tackle their goals, overcome obstacles, and celebrate their victories reignites your own drive. Their encouragement reminds you of your initial motivation and keeps you focused, even when the path appears challenging.

Acting: Your Path to Financial Mastery

You now have the knowledge, tools, and systems to *Grow, Multiply, and Protect* your wealth. But knowing is not enough, acting is what creates lasting change.

Here's your next step: Commit to implement what you've learned.

Start by choosing one immediate action from each of the three Wealth Accelerators:

- Grow — Define your next financial goal and create an Intentional Spending Plan to align your money with your values.
- Multiply — Set up or increase automated investments, ensuring your money works for you.
- Protect — Meet with an advisor or begin estate planning to safeguard your financial future.

The biggest mistake people make is assuming they'll "get to it later." But later often turns into never. The moment to start is now.

To make this process easier, the *Law Mother app* provides:

- Interactive versions of the tools in this book.
- Direct access to vetted advisors, estate planners, and tax strategists.
- A community of like-minded individuals to support and hold you accountable.

Log in today and take your first step toward lifelong financial security.

YOUR WEALTHY EVER AFTER STARTS TODAY

Wealth isn't just about money. It's about *freedom*. It's about **security**. It's about breaking cycles and creating a future where you and your family are no longer just getting by, you're thriving.

I know what it feels like to wonder if financial peace is even possible.

I started my law firm with a 0% interest credit card, not knowing if it would work. A few months later, I found out I was pregnant. Then the world shut down. I could have let fear win. I could have stayed stuck in survival mode. But I made a choice. **I chose to take control**.

And that choice changed everything.

Now, it's your turn.

- You don't have to be perfect.
- You don't need to know everything.
- You must *start*.

Because here's the truth: *wealth doesn't wait*. The more time you spend hesitating; the more opportunities slip away.

So, what will you do today?

Will you finally organize your finances?

Will you take the first step toward investing?

Will you put protections in place, so your family is never unprepared?

You have everything you need, the knowledge, the strategies, the tools. **Now, you need to act**.

Scan the QR code to FREE access the Law Mother app and start building your legacy today.

Your future self, the financially free one, in control, and building generational wealth, is waiting. Please don't keep them waiting any longer.

APPENDIX A: HOW TO REPROGRAM
YOUR MONEY BELIEFS

Unlocking Subconscious Beliefs with NLP and Self-Hypnosis

The tools of self-coaching we explored earlier laid the foundation for building awareness, helping you identify and process emotions that influence your financial decisions. Now, we're going one step further. This section dives even deeper into the hidden forces that shape your relationship with money.

At the core of self-coaching lies the idea that change begins with understanding yourself. But sometimes, the beliefs driving your actions aren't always obvious. They live below the surface, in your subconscious, quietly guiding your choices without you even realizing it. Techniques like Neuro-Linguistic Programming (NLP) and self-hypnosis come in here. These powerful tools help you uncover and reprogram those deeply ingrained patterns, taking your self-coaching practice to the next level.

Whether you're working on overcoming fear, rewriting money stories, or building confidence in your financial decisions, NLP and self-hypnosis open doors to transformation. They don't just help you manage the emotions we've discussed, they empower you to change the beliefs that fuel them. Together, these techniques allow you to reshape your mindset, align your actions with your goals, and become a version of yourself who thrives with money.

Now, let's explore how subconscious beliefs are formed, how they appear in our lives, and how you can begin unlocking their power.

Discovering Subconscious Beliefs

Subconscious beliefs are like invisible strings, quietly guiding the decisions and actions we take every day. These beliefs are often formed early in life, shaped by our families, experiences, or even cultural narratives about money. Without us realizing, they can steer us toward choices that aren't always in our best interest.

For example, you might believe, "I'll never be good with money," or "I have to work hard for every dollar." Maybe you've internalized the idea that "money is the root of all problems." These beliefs don't just live in your mind, they can show up in your behavior, causing you to overspend, avoid creating a financial plan or pass up opportunities to grow your wealth. They're sneaky, but they don't have to stay that way.

Rewiring Beliefs with NLP

Neuro-linguistic programming, or NLP, is a way to reprogram the mind by changing how you think and talk about your experiences. It works by examining the language you use, both in your thoughts and out loud, and helping you create new patterns that support your goals.

One powerful NLP technique is called anchoring. Think of it as creating a shortcut to a positive emotional state. For instance, imagine feeling confident every time you make a financial decision. You could anchor that feeling by recalling a past moment of success, focusing on the emotional energy, and associating it with a simple action like touching your wrist. Over time, you train your brain to recreate that confident feeling whenever needed.

Another technique you can use is reframing. Instead of telling yourself, "I can't save money," try swapping it for something more empowering, like, "I'm learning to build my savings." It might initially feel awkward, it's normal for old beliefs to fight back. Start small by writing down a limiting belief about money. Then challenge it by asking, "Is this true? What's another way I could look at this?" Replace that belief with one that serves you and make it part of your daily self-talk.

The Power of Self-Hypnosis

If NLP involves actively engaging with your thoughts, then self-hypnosis resembles the act of planting seeds of change directly into your subconscious. By achieving a deep state of relaxation, you can bypass the resistance of your conscious mind and instill supportive beliefs where they have the greatest impact, at the core of your self-perception.

I strongly believe in the power of self-hypnosis because of my father. My father introduced me to it when I was just a little girl. He had a collection of self-hypnosis cassette tapes that he would play to help me fall asleep. Some nights, he would guide me through relaxation exercises, using his calm voice to create vivid, soothing visualizations as I drifted off to sleep.

One childhood memory stands out vividly. As a young girl, I fell off my bike, badly breaking my arm and dislocating two bones. The pain was excruciating, and by the time we reached the ER, I was sobbing hysterically. The nurses warned my father that they would need to reset the bones manually, which would be intense for both of us to endure. However, my dad remained calm and asked me to close my eyes. In the emergency room, he guided me through a visualization to help me relax. He had me envision a peaceful, safe place where my body felt light and at ease. Within minutes, I stopped crying. The nurses were shocked at how quickly I calmed down, but my dad was not.

Now, as an adult, self-hypnosis remains a valuable tool in my life. I use it regularly to help me fall asleep on restless nights, challenge and overcome my limiting beliefs, and prepare for major milestones like childbirth. During my pregnancy, guided self-hypnosis exercises became part of my routine, assisting me in releasing fear and focusing on building confidence in my body's strength for labor.

The beauty of self-hypnosis lies in its versatility. Whether it's rewiring negative thought patterns, easing anxiety, or simply finding a moment of calm amidst chaos, it is a tool anyone can learn to use. If you're new to this, don't worry, I've included some beginner-friendly exercises in this section that you can try independently. Hiring a professional specializing in guided hypnosis can be a fantastic option for those seeking deeper guidance or struggling to get started.

Your mind is a powerful ally, able to transform how you experience both minor and major moments in your life. With practice and intention, self-hypnosis can turn into a life-changing tool, just as it has for me.

To practice self-hypnosis, find a quiet space where you won't be interrupted. Close your eyes and take several slow, deep breaths. Once you feel calm, visualize a specific goal, such as building a $5,000 peace of mind fund. Imagine every detail of that moment when you have achieved it. How does it feel? What do you say to yourself? Allow that sense of pride and accomplishment to fill you. Repeat a positive affirmation, such as, "I am confident and capable of creating wealth," letting it resonate as you focus on your breath. Just 5 to 10 minutes of practice can help you begin shifting your beliefs over time.

Transforming Beliefs in Real Life

This process of rewiring the subconscious isn't just theoretical, it's life-changing. For instance, consider a person who transitioned from believing, "Money is stressful," to affirming, "I manage my money with ease." That shift didn't occur overnight; rather, through gentle daily changes, they eventually stopped avoiding their finances. Instead, they created a realistic budget that suited their lives.

Imagine someone who always felt terrified of investing. By replacing their fear with "I can start small and learn as I go," they took their first steps, researching and gradually building confidence in their choices. Each step diminished some of the fear, and every small success reinforced their belief in their ability to grow.

Understanding Your Own Beliefs

The good news is that you don't have to remain stuck in the stories your mind has told you. Begin by reflecting on the beliefs you hold about money. What examples were modeled for you growing up? How do those beliefs manifest in your actions now? Journaling can help illuminate these thoughts, as can mindfulness, where you observe how thoughts arise without judgment.

The key to long-lasting transformation is consistency. Whether you're practicing self-coaching, NLP, self-hypnosis, or a combination, returning to these tools regularly will build momentum. These techniques enable you to break free from cycles of self-sabotage and progress toward a financial future that aligns with your goals.

Every emotion, every belief is a chance to grow and reimagine what's possible for you. By unlocking these subconscious patterns, you gain clarity and confidence needed to create the life you deserve. And that's where the real transformation begins.

Finishing the Story: How Reprogramming Changed My Money Reality

Do you remember the day when my bonus didn't come through? The moment I sat at my kitchen table, trying to convince myself that I wouldn't fail? That was when I realized I couldn't afford to wait for *someday* to get serious about money.

I'd love to tell you that today, I'm perfect. I'm not.

I'm a lot happier and a lot more at peace. For example, I exercise to stay in shape and practice financial and mindset skills to stay in financial shape.

I still have financial challenges that will trigger me, like when a business decision cost me $100,000 last year. The end goal isn't perfection. Life is a journey.

The goal is to enjoy your life journey. Enjoy your successes, including your financial growth and your wealthy ever after!

Mastering your money mindset involves awareness, acceptance, and creating a new mindset with the right tools. The more you practice awareness of your thoughts and emotions, accept your current patterns without judgment, and intentionally shift your beliefs, the more control you'll gain over your financial future.

APPENDIX B: INVESTING 101

INVESTING BASICS (BUILDING THE FOUNDATION)

Understanding the fundamentals of investing is the first step toward creating a stable and successful financial future. This section will help you grasp the essentials, from public investments to the intricacies of stocks, bonds, and mutual funds, using relatable examples to clarify these concepts. By the end, you will have the confidence to take your initial steps into the investing world.

What Are Public Investments?

Public investments include assets like stocks, bonds, and mutual funds, which are available to individual and institutional investors through markets like stock exchanges. These investments are known for their accessibility, transparency, and liquidity, as investors can easily buy or sell them.

Example: When you purchase shares of Apple (AAPL), you're making a public investment in a publicly traded company available on the stock market.

Public investments generally provide long-term capital growth, income generation, and diversification opportunities. They are accessible to investors of all levels, making them a practical means for anyone to create wealth.

Public investments have historically outperformed savings accounts in the long run through compounded growth in investments like index funds or dividend-paying stocks.

Passive Investing

A passive investment strategy involves minimal buying and selling and focuses on long-term growth. Index funds and ETFs, which mirror the performance of market indices like the S&P 500, are popular choices for passive investors. They are cost-effective and require less time to manage.

Example: You can benefit from the overall market's performance, with lower fees and effort, by investing in an S&P 500 ETF.

Active Investing

Active investors seek to outperform the market by researching and selecting specific stocks, bonds, or funds. While this strategy can lead to higher returns, it also involves higher costs, effort, and risks due to frequent trading.

Example: Actively trading technology stocks during market rallies to generate above-average returns.

What Is the Stock Market?

The stock market is a network of exchanges where investors buy and sell company ownership shares. It enables companies to raise capital while allowing individuals to grow their wealth.

Exchanges such as the New York Stock Exchange (NYSE) or Nasdaq enable the trading of stocks in companies like Amazon and Tesla.

Individual Stocks

Buying individual stocks means owning a portion of a single company, making your returns reliant on that company's performance. This offers higher reward potential but also greater risk.

Example: Purchasing shares of Microsoft (MSFT) means your investment depends solely on Microsoft's business performance.

Funds

Funds such as mutual funds or ETFs pool investors' money to buy a diversified selection of stocks. This reduces risk by spreading your investment across multiple companies.

Example: A technology ETF might include shares of multiple companies, such as Apple, Microsoft, and Google, offering diversification in a single purchase.

What Affects Stock Prices?

Stock prices are influenced by supply and demand. Factors such as company earnings, industry trends, macroeconomic conditions, and global events can also drive stock price changes.

Common Misconceptions About Stock Investing

Myth: You need to be wealthy to invest.
Fact: Many brokerages allow you to invest as little as $10 using fractional shares.

Myth: All stocks are risky.
Fact: While individual stocks can be volatile, investing in diversified funds is less risky. For example, utility funds are considered stable and predictable income-producing investments because people and companies consistently need necessities like energy and water. Moreover, utility funds generally provide dividends, which are considered to be similar to interest on a bank account in terms of providing a pretty consistent flow of cash to the investor.

Risk vs. Reward: Understanding Volatility

Stock market investing involves balancing risk and reward. While stocks historically offer higher returns than bonds or savings accounts, they are subject to volatility.

Example: During market downturns, stock prices may plummet, but patient investors benefit as markets recover.

Actionable Tip: If you're risk-averse, consider allocating a larger portion of your portfolio to index funds instead of individual stocks.

Bonds

Bonds are another critical type of public investment that complements stocks by offering stability and income generation, especially during periods of market volatility.

What Are Bonds, and How Do They Work?

A bond is a loan you offer to a company, municipality, or government in exchange for interest payments and the return of your principal investment upon maturity. They are considered fixed-income investments due to their predictable payments.

Example: Buying a $1,000 U.S. Treasury bond means lending money to the government, which will pay you interest until the bond matures.

Types of Bonds

Government Bonds: Issued by national governments. Considered the safest type of bond, like U.S. Treasury bonds.

Municipal Bonds: Issued by local or state governments, offering tax advantages on interest earnings.

Corporate Bonds: Issued by companies; higher yield potential but greater risk than government bonds.

High-Yield Bonds: Offered by lower-rated companies. Also known as "junk bonds," these carry higher risks but offer better returns.

How Bond Interest (Coupons) Work

Bonds pay investors regular interest, known as coupons, usually semi-annually or annually. The interest rate is predetermined and expressed as a percentage of the bond's face value.

Example: A $1,000 bond with a 5% annual coupon rate pays $50 in interest each year until maturity.

Bonds vs. Stocks: When to Invest in Each

Bonds offer a steady income stream and are less volatile, making them ideal during economic downturns or for retirees seeking stability.

Conversely, stocks are better suited for long-term growth and are favored by younger investors with higher risk tolerance.

Actionable Tip: A balanced portfolio may include bonds and stocks for growth and stability. For instance, as you near retirement, shift your allocation from 70% stocks and 30% bonds to a 50/50 split.

Bond Risks

Inflation Risk: Rising inflation reduces the purchasing power of bond interest payments.

Interest Rate Risk: Existing bond prices typically fall when interest rates rise.

Credit Risk: Lower-rated issuers may default on their bond payments. Always check credit ratings from agencies like Moody's or Standard & Poor's before investing. These ratings range from AAA, the highest rating indicating lowest risk, to AA, low risk, contrasted with higher risks bond ratings at BB and below, which are generally not recommended for casual investors.

Mutual Funds

Mutual funds are collective investments managed by professionals who pool money from numerous investors to purchase various assets. These funds simplify the process of diversifying your investments.

- **What Are Mutual Funds?**

  Imagine a basket filled with 50 different fruits. Some fruits (assets) may spoil (lose value), but the others help ensure the basket retains its overall worth. Similarly, mutual funds diversify your money across various stocks or bonds to minimize risk.

- **Active vs. Passive Management Example:**

  » *Active Management:* Jane invests in a Technology Growth Fund managed by experts who actively adjust the fund's holdings to outperform the tech market. This approach involves higher fees but leverages the expert or team of experts' insights and strategies.

  » *Passive Management:* Meanwhile, Sam chooses an S&P 500 Index Fund, which is passively managed and tracks 500 large U.S. companies. It's low-cost and grows in line with the market, requiring minimal intervention.

- **Expense Ratios:**

  One critical factor to consider with mutual funds is their expense ratios. The fund charges these annual fees for managing your investments. For instance, if a mutual fund delivers an annual return of 7% but charges a 2% expense ratio, your net return is reduced to just 5%. While this might not seem significant in a single year, high fees can erode tens or even hundreds of thousands of dollars from your returns over decades.

A Word of Caution on Fees

Always evaluate the expense ratios of the funds you are considering. Actively managed mutual funds generally have higher fees than passive funds like index funds or exchange-traded funds (ETFs). High fees do not guarantee better performance, and in many cases, actively managed funds do not consistently outperform their passive counterparts.

For instance, Maria chooses between an actively managed mutual fund with a 1.5% expense ratio and an index fund with a 0.2% expense ratio. After 20 years, with a $10,000 investment and an average return of 7%, the index fund would grow to approximately $38,700, whereas the actively managed fund would only reach about $31,400 after fees. This results in a difference of over $7,000, a significant amount for any investor.

Why Index Funds and ETFs Can Be Better Alternatives

- **Lower Expense Ratios**

  Index funds and ETFs usually have much lower fees than mutual funds. For example, many broad-market index funds that track the S&P 500 have expense ratios as low as 0.03%. This means more of your money remains invested and compounds over time.

- **Diversification at a Low Cost**

  Like mutual funds, these Index Funds and ETFs distribute your investments among various stocks or bonds, but they achieve this without the high fees associated with active management.

- **Flexibility and Liquidity**

  ETFs, in particular, trade like stocks, offering a convenient option for those who want to buy or sell shares throughout the trading day.

For cost-conscious investors, these lower-fee alternatives can be a smart choice. By directing a substantial portion of your portfolio toward low-cost index funds and ETFs, you're developing a strategy that's both efficient and aligned with long-term wealth growth.

Common Investment Mistakes and How to Avoid Them

Even experienced investors fall into traps that can derail their progress. Being aware of these mistakes can save you money and stress.

- **Emotional Investing**

  Many investors buy at market highs, fearing they'll miss out on gains, and sell at lows, panicking during declines. For example, during the 2008 financial crisis, millions of investors sold their assets at a loss, only to see the market rebound a few years later. Stick to your long-term plan and remember that markets fluctuate.

- **Chasing Hot Stocks or Trends**

  Investors often flock to hot stocks or sectors, only to see those investments fade. For instance, while tech stocks surged during the dot-com bubble, many crashed soon after. Instead, diversify your portfolio and avoid over-concentrating in one area.

- **Overpaying in Fees**

  High fees in mutual funds or frequent trading can eat into your returns. Use tools to compare expense ratios and look for cost-efficient options like index funds or ETFs.

- **Neglecting Rebalancing**

  Over time, your portfolio can drift from its original allocation, increasing risk exposure. Rebalancing involves realigning your portfolio with your targeted mix of stocks, bonds, and other assets.

- **Ignoring the Impact of Inflation**

  Inflation diminishes the purchasing power of your money. An investment that earns a 2% return in a year with 3% inflation effectively loses value. To surpass inflation, prioritize investments with greater growth potential, such as equities.

Creating Your Personalized Public Investment Strategy

Developing a strategy tailored to your goals ensures that your money works efficiently for you.

- **Aligning Investments with Financial Goals**

  Are you saving for retirement, a child's education, or a home? Each goal may require different investment approaches.
  For example:
  - » Retirement (long-term): Increase stock allocation for growth.
  - » Education (medium-term): Use a mix of bonds and index funds for stability and reasonable returns.

> » House down payment (short-term): Focus on low-risk options like high-yield savings accounts or short-term bonds or utility funds.

- **Deciding on Risk Tolerance and Time Horizons**

  Your capacity to manage risk and the timeframe before you need the funds should shape your investment portfolio. You can endure stock market fluctuations if you're 30 and have decades until retirement. If you're over 55, you may want to transition toward bonds for more stability.

- **Steps to Build a Lifestyle-Aligned Portfolio**

  1. Assess your goals, financial situation, and risk tolerance.
  2. Choose a mix of stocks, bonds, ETFs, or mutual funds that aligns with your objectives.
  3. Diversify your investments to reduce risk across multiple sectors and geographies.

- **Importance of Reviewing and Adjusting Strategy Regularly**

  Life changes, and so should your investment plan. Review your portfolio at least annually to rebalance it, consider changes in your goals, and ensure you're on track to meet them.

You can build a strong financial future by avoiding common mistakes and tailoring your investment strategy to your life. Investing isn't about luck or timing the market; it's about discipline, knowledge, and commitment to your goals.

REITREMENT INVESTMENT ACCOUNTS: UNDERSTANDING INDIVIDUAL, EMPLOYER-SPONSOERED AND SPECIALTY RETIREMENT

ACCOUNTS AND ANNUITIES

Individual Retirement Accounts

Saving for retirement is one of the most important financial goals, and individual retirement accounts (IRAs) offer diverse options to suit various needs.

What Is a Roth IRA?

A Roth IRA is a retirement account where contributions are made with after-tax dollars. This means the money grows tax-free, and qualified withdrawals in retirement are also tax-free.

Tax-Free Growth and Penalty-Free Withdrawals:

The main advantage of a Roth IRA is that your savings grow tax-free over time. Additionally, withdrawals in retirement (age 59½ or older) are penalty- and tax-free, offering significant financial flexibility in your golden years.

Flexibility for Emergencies:

You can withdraw your contributions (not the earnings) to a Roth IRA at any time, without penalties, making it a useful backup for emergencies.

Example: If you contribute $6,000 annually for five years, you'd have $30,000 in contributions available if you need it before retirement without incurring any penalties.

Example of Wealth Accumulation Through Early Contributions:

Starting young makes a huge difference thanks to compounding. If you contribute $6,000 annually to your Roth IRA starting at age 25 and earn an average 7% annual return, you could accumulate nearly $1 million by retirement age.

What Is a Backdoor Roth IRA?

This strategy is designed for high earners whose income exceeds the limits for direct Roth IRA contributions.

Overview:

A Backdoor Roth IRA allows you to indirectly contribute to a Roth IRA by first contributing to a traditional IRA and then converting those funds to a Roth IRA.

Steps to Execute Efficiently:

Contribute to a traditional IRA.

Quickly convert the contribution to a Roth IRA to minimize tax liability.

Avoid leaving untaxed earnings in the traditional IRA before conversion to keep the process clean and minimize taxes.

SEP IRAs and SIMPLE IRAs

SEP IRA (Simplified Employee Pension): Ideal for self-employed individuals and small business owners. Contributions come from the employer (not employees) and offer a higher annual contribution limit than traditional IRAs.

SIMPLE IRA (Savings Incentive Match Plan for Employees): A retirement plan for small businesses with fewer than 100 employees. Employers match contributions or contribute a fixed percentage of employee pay, making it a straightforward option for small organizations.

Employer Sponsored Retirement Accounts

Employer-sponsored retirement accounts often provide valuable incentives such as matches or tax advantages. Here's what you need to know about these plans.

401(k)s and 403(b)s

401(k): A popular option for private-sector employees, these accounts allow for tax-deferred contributions that grow until retirement. Many employers offer matching contributions, adding "free money" to your savings.

Example: If your employer matches 50% of the first 6% of your salary you contribute, aim to save at least that 6% to maximize the match.

403(b): Like a 401(k), but available for employees of public schools, non-profits, and certain government organizations. These may also include special provisions like annuity-based options.

457(b)s

These are retirement accounts for government and some non-profit employees. The key advantage is that you can contribute to a 457(b) and a 401(k) or 403(b) simultaneously, doubling your savings potential.

Thrift Savings Plan (TSPs)

TSPs are available to federal employees and members of the military. These plans offer low-cost investment options and a federal contribution match, making them highly efficient for growing retirement savings.

Pensions

Pensions provide guaranteed income in retirement but are increasingly rare. As pension benefits are often tied to tenure, they're best for individuals anticipating long-term employment with one employer.

When to Use and Avoid Employer Accounts

Use: When employers offer matching contributions or low-fee plan options. Always prioritize free money in the form of matches.

Avoid: If the plan has high administrative fees or limited investment options, you may want to contribute only up to the match and focus on other accounts like an IRA.

Specialty Retirement Accounts

Solo 401(k)

Designed for self-employed individuals and business owners with no employees, Solo 401(k)s allow for employee and employer contributions, significantly increasing savings potential within a single plan.

Self-Directed IRA

A Self-Directed IRA gives you more control over investment choices, such as real estate or private equity, which are not commonly available in conventional accounts. Be cautious of the increased complexity and risk associated with these investments.

Defined Pension Plans

Defined pension plans offer fixed benefits at retirement based on salary and tenure. They are typically used by small business owners who want high contributions toward retirement.

Annuities

Annuities can provide a dependable income stream during retirement, making them attractive for those concerned about outliving their savings. However, they come with fees and restrictions, so it's essential to evaluate them carefully.

Importance of Reviewing and Adjusting Strategy:

Revise your annuity contracts to ensure they align with your evolving financial priorities. For instance, you might roll over some annuities into new vehicles with lower fees or different payout structures.

BRINGING IT ALL TOGETHER

Retirement planning offers a variety of account options, each catering to different needs and stages of life. You can create a robust and diversified retirement plan by combining IRAs, employer-sponsored accounts, specialty options, and potentially annuities. Start by taking advantage of employer matches, adding the flexibility of an IRA, and layering in advanced strategies like backdoor Roth IRAs or self-directed accounts when appropriate. Adjust your plans as you approach retirement to reflect your changing priorities and ensure a comfortable, secure future.

Avoiding Common Retirement Account Mistakes

Retirement accounts are powerful tools for building long-term wealth, but they must be used effectively to unlock their full potential. Mistakes in handling these accounts can cost you years of progress and tens of thousands of dollars. Here's how to avoid some of the most common pitfalls:

1. Not Actively Choosing Investments in Retirement Accounts

One of the biggest mistakes people make is assuming their retirement account will grow independently without actively selecting investments. When you open a 401(k) or IRA, your contributions often sit in a default fund, like a money market account or a target-date fund. While these may provide stability, they might not grow your savings aggressively enough to meet your retirement goals.

- Example: Sarah signs up for her company's 401(k) but doesn't choose any specific investments. Her contributions default to a money market fund earning just 1% annually. Over 30 years, her $10,000 yearly contributions would grow to around $348,000. If instead, she had chosen an S&P 500 Index Fund (with an average annual growth of 7%), her balance could grow to over $1 million.
- Actionable Advice: Review the investment options offered within your retirement account. Diversify your investments across stocks, bonds, and funds that align with your goals and risk tolerance. If unsure, consider speaking to a financial advisor or using target-date funds geared toward your expected retirement year.

2. Not Maximizing Contributions to Tax-Advantaged Accounts

Retirement accounts like 401(k)s, Roth IRAs, and traditional IRAs offer significant tax benefits, but failing to maximize contributions to these accounts means you're leaving money on the table. These tax advantages allow your wealth to compound more effectively over time.

- Example: John contributes just $5,000 annually to his Roth IRA, even though he's eligible to contribute up to the maximum limit of $6,000 (2023). Over 30 years with a 7% return, this $1,000 difference each year results in a missed opportunity of over $100,000 in potential savings.
- Actionable Advice:
  - » Aim to contribute as much as possible to your retirement accounts, starting with employer-sponsored accounts like a 401(k), especially if there's an employer match (always aim to contribute enough to get the full match; it's free money).
  - » After contributing enough to receive your match, focus on adding to a Roth IRA or Traditional IRA, maxing out contributions if possible.
  - » If funds are tight, start small and increase your contributions whenever you get a raise or bonus. Even small, incremental increases can add up over time.

3. Early Withdrawals and Their Impact on Compounding Growth

Taking money out of retirement accounts early may seem tempting during financial hardship, but it can derail your long-term savings. You will face immediate penalties and taxes (if you're under age 59½) and lose out on the compounding growth that makes retirement accounts so powerful.

- Example: Mark withdraws $10,000 from his 401(k) at age 35 to cover credit card debt. After paying a 10% penalty and taxes, he's left with just $7,000. More importantly, that $10,000 could have grown to about $76,000 by retirement at age 65, assuming a 7% return. His decision cost him nearly $70,000 in potential savings.
- Actionable Advice:
  - » Avoid withdrawing from retirement accounts before age 59½ unless it's an absolute emergency or you qualify for an exemption (e.g., first-time homebuyer, education expenses for IRAs).

» Build an emergency fund with 3-6 months of living expenses to prevent the need for early withdrawals.

» If you leave an employer, don't cash out your 401(k). Instead, roll it over into an IRA or your new employer's plan to preserve the tax benefits and compounding potential.

Bringing It All Together

Leveraging retirement accounts effectively requires active participation. Make informed investment choices, contribute as much as possible to tax-advantaged accounts, and protect your savings from early withdrawals. By avoiding these common mistakes, you'll set yourself on a path to a more stable and prosperous retirement. Every small step you take today can make a big difference in your financial future!

The Importance of Diversifying Investments

Diversification minimizes the impact of any single poor-performing investment on your overall portfolio. Financial markets can be unpredictable, and spreading your assets helps stabilize your growth. For example, if you put all your money into tech stocks and the sector experiences a downturn, your entire portfolio could suffer. Diversification acts as a safety net, reducing risk while preserving your potential for gains.

Building a Diversified Portfolio

A diversified portfolio is the backbone of any successful investment strategy. By spreading your money across different asset types, industries, and geographies, you can reduce the risk of significant losses while increasing the potential for long-term returns. Here's how to structure and maintain a diversified portfolio based on age, risk tolerance, and financial goals.

1. Balancing Investments According to Age and Risk Tolerance

Your age and risk tolerance play a significant role in allocating your investments. Here's a closer look at how you can balance your portfolio at different stages of life:

- Younger Investors Focus on Growth

  Younger investors have more time to recover from market fluctuations, which means they can take on higher risks for potentially higher rewards. Equities (stocks) are popular for younger investors because they historically provide strong long-term growth.

  » *Example:* If Lena is 25 and invests $10,000 in an S&P 500 Index Fund with an average annual return of 7%, her investment could grow to over $70,000 by age 55. Stocks offer the growth potential she needs to build wealth over decades.

- Older Investors Lean Toward Stability

  As investors approach retirement, preserving wealth becomes more important than aggressive growth. Older investors often shift a portion of their portfolio into less volatile assets like bonds, real estate, or dividend-paying stocks.

  » *Example:* At 55, William might allocate 60% of his portfolio to bonds and stable income-producing assets while keeping 40% in stocks to outpace inflation. This balance provides some growth while reducing the risk of major losses as he nears retirement.

- Actionable Advice

  Use the "Rule of 110" to determine your stock allocation. Subtract your age from 110 to find the percentage of your portfolio in stocks. For example:

  » A 30-year-old could invest 80% in stocks and 20% in bonds or safer assets.

  » A 60-year-old might aim for 50% stocks and 50% bonds. Adjust these percentages based on your risk tolerance.

2. The Principle of Diversification

The saying "don't put all your eggs in one basket" rings especially true in investing. While one type of investment might perform exceptionally well one year, it could underperform the next. Diversifying across asset classes, industries, and regions minimizes this risk.

- Avoid Putting All Your Eggs in One Basket

  A portfolio heavily invested in a single company or sector is highly vulnerable to downturns. For instance, during the 2008 financial crisis, investors heavily reliant on real estate lost significant portions of their wealth when the housing market collapsed. Diversification can protect you from such concentrated risks.

- Strategies for Diversification Across Asset Types
  1. Mix Asset Classes: Combine stocks, bonds, real estate, and cash-equivalents to spread risk.
     » Stocks for growth.
     » Bonds for stability.
     » Real estate for inflation protection.
     » Cash equivalents for liquidity.
  2. Diversify Geographically: Exposure to international markets can protect you from regional downturns. For example, if U.S. markets decline, investments in European or Asian markets might offset the losses.
     » *Example:* A Global Index Fund gives you exposure to companies across different continents.
  3. Diversify Within Each Asset Class: Even within stocks, diversify across industries like tech, healthcare, and utilities. Sector-specific ETFs can help achieve this balance.

- Actionable Advice
  » Use Funds and ETFs: Index funds and ETFs are naturally diversified. For example, an S&P 500 Index Fund spreads investments across 500 companies in various industries.

» Limit Individual Stock Exposure: Avoid having more than 5-10% of your portfolio in any single stock to minimize concentration risk.

» Rebalance Regularly: Over time, some investments will outperform others, causing your portfolio allocation to shift. Rebalancing ensures you stick to your plan. For instance, if your stocks grow from 60% to 70% of your portfolio, sell some of the stock and reinvest in bonds or other assets to maintain your desired balance.

Bringing It All Together

Building a diversified portfolio is essential for managing risk and achieving consistent growth. Younger investors can take advantage of equities to maximize long-term gains, while older investors should focus on stability through bonds and other low-risk investments. By diversifying across asset types, industries, and regions, you're better equipped to weather market fluctuations and achieve your financial goals. Remember, diversification doesn't guarantee against losses, but it significantly reduces your risk exposure. Regularly review and rebalance your portfolio to align with your evolving goals and life circumstances.

APPENDIX C: FINANCIAL ALIGNMENT CHECKLIST FOR COUPLES

FINANCIAL ALIGNMENT CHECKLIST FOR COUPLES

Use this checklist to ensure you and your spouse are on the same page financially. Go through each section together and check off completed items.

1. ***Understanding Each Other's Money Mindset***
   - Discuss how money was handled in each of your families growing up.
   - Identify if you are more of a spender or saver, risk-taker or security-driven.
   - Share any financial fears, anxieties, or past money mistakes.

2. ***Full Financial Transparency***
   - Share all income sources (salaries, side hustles, passive income).
   - List all debts (credit cards, loans, mortgages).
   - Review savings, investments, and retirement accounts.
   - Discuss current monthly expenses and spending habits.

3. Setting Shared Financial Goals

- Agree on short-term goals (budgeting, debt payoff, upcoming expenses).
- Define mid-term goals (home purchase, vacations, children's education).
- Align on long-term goals (retirement, generational wealth, legacy planning).

4. Structuring Your Finances as a Team

- Decide on joint vs. separate accounts (Yours, Mine, Ours approach).
- Automate savings, investing, and bill payments.
- Allocate personal "fun money" for individual spending freedom.
- Set a schedule for regular "Money Check-Ins" (weekly, monthly, or quarterly).

5. Handling Financial Disagreements

- Establish a spending threshold where purchases require joint approval.
- Agree on an approach for managing unexpected expenses.
- Outline how you'll compromise on investment and risk decisions.
- Commit to revisiting and adjusting your plan as needed.

6. Protecting Your Financial Future

- Ensure both partners have a will and estate plan in place.
- Review and update life insurance and beneficiary designations.
- Create an Opportunity Fund (3-6 months of expenses).
- Discuss financial plans for aging parents or dependents.

Final Step: Your Money Alignment Action Plan

- Set a date for your next financial check-in.
- Choose one immediate action to improve your financial alignment.
- Celebrate being proactive about your financial future.

APPENDIX D: YOUR TRUE LEGACY

VALUES, INSIGHTS, AND STORIES

An estate plan isn't just about dollars, legal documents, or dividing up possessions. While those things matter, your true legacy lies in the values you live by, the lessons you've learned, and the stories that define your family's identity. Alongside financial assets, these intangible treasures are what truly leave an enduring impact on future generations.

Passing On More Than Wealth

From the wisdom shared around your dinner table to the traditions that bring your family together, these are the things that will echo through time far beyond material wealth. Your insights and personal stories serve as a compass for your children and grandchildren, offering guidance and connection, even when you're no longer there to share them in person.

Leaving your family with a record of what truly matters, your values, memories, and life philosophies, cultivates deeper bonds. It's about saying, "This is what I stood for, and this is what I hope for you." This kind of legacy can be built intentionally and lovingly, and it becomes a powerful complement to the financial preparation you've made.

Tools to Capture Your Legacy

Creating a space for your values and stories in your estate plan may feel overwhelming, but it doesn't have to be. Here are practical ways to capture and share your heart's wealth with your loved ones:

- **Write a Legacy Letter**

  A legacy letter is a deeply personal way to express your hopes, dreams, and reflections for your family. This could be a letter to your children or grandchildren, sharing what you've learned about life, what you hope they'll cherish, and even stories from your own experiences that shaped your principles. It's an opportunity to provide inspiration and comfort in their lives for years to come.

- **Create a Family Mission Statement**

  Families, like businesses, thrive on shared purpose. A family mission statement outlines the core values and goals you want to pass down to your descendants. Perhaps it's a commitment to lifelong learning, a focus on helping others, or traditions that define your family's culture. Draft this as a family, allowing each generation to contribute, so everyone feels connected to it.

- **Record Family Histories and Lessons**

  Consider recording interviews with loved ones or writing down pivotal family stories. How did your family overcome challenges in the past? What character traits helped you achieve success? These narratives are rich resources for future generations to learn from and draw strength.

- **Establish a Philanthropic Legacy**

  Passing on values often goes hand in hand with giving back. Establishing a charitable giving plan in your estate can guide your heirs to continue supporting causes close to your heart. By involving them in the planning process, you actively share the importance of generosity.

Insights from Legally Ever After

The book *Legally Ever After* reminds us that legacies are built not only through what we leave behind but also through the intentions that guide those actions. It encourages families to consider questions like, "What stories do we want our children to repeat to their children?" or "How can we ensure our legacy stands for something greater than ourselves?"

One particularly moving insight is the idea that wealth alone doesn't keep families united, shared values and purpose do. Many individuals who prioritize value-driven estate planning report that their families feel closer, more connected, and grateful for the clarity they've inherited along with financial resources.

Building a Legacy That Lasts

Your true legacy is the immortal part of your story, values and insights that will guide, inspire, and bring comfort to future generations. To start this process today, consider combining your financial and emotional legacies by speaking with your family, writing a reflective letter, or capturing your stories on paper or video.

By taking these steps, you're doing more than planning for what happens tomorrow, you're strengthening your family's foundation and ensuring that your memory will continue to enrich lives for years to come. Your estate plan is a gift, but your values and stories are a treasure to pass on. Start shaping this meaningful legacy today.

Financially Educating Kids to Become Stewards of Generational Wealth

Building a legacy isn't just about protecting assets, it's about preparing your children to manage, sustain, and grow the wealth you've worked so hard to create. Financial education is a critical part of this process. When you teach your kids to understand and respect the value of money, you empower them to become responsible stewards of generational wealth. This education doesn't just preserve wealth; it ensures that your family's financial legacy is aligned with your values and benefits future generations.

Why Financial Literacy Matters

Many families lose generational wealth within a few decades because heirs are unprepared to manage it. Financial literacy is the key to breaking this cycle. By instilling the principles of budgeting, investing, and responsible spending, you're not only giving your children the tools to thrive financially, you're also showing them how to contribute to the family's long-term success.

Insights from *Legally Ever After* highlight that wealth stewardship requires more than just knowledge of financial concepts. It's about fostering a sense of responsibility, purpose, and a deeper understanding of the mission behind the wealth itself. When kids recognize that family wealth is rooted in shared goals and values, they're better equipped to honor and build upon it.

Practical Steps to Educate and Empower

Start small but start early. The earlier you begin weaving financial lessons into everyday life, the more natural and meaningful the process will feel for your children. Here are some practical ways to nurture strong financial habits:

- **Introduce Age-Appropriate Lessons**

  Start with simple concepts when your kids are young. Teach them the value of saving by encouraging them to set aside a portion of their allowance. You can use visual tools like jars to represent saving, spending, and giving. As they grow older, build on these basics with lessons about managing bank accounts, earning interest, and budgeting their expenses.

- **Set Up Savings or Investment Accounts**

  Open savings or custodial investment accounts in your child's name to teach them how money grows over time. Show them how their contributions, combined with compound interest, can work toward long-term goals like starting a business, buying a home, or pursuing higher education.

- **Share Family Financial Goals**

  Bring your children into the conversation about the family's financial vision. Outline what you're working toward, for example, paying off the mortgage, contributing to a cause close to your heart, or funding future family endeavors. By including your kids in these discussions, you help them understand the purpose behind financial decisions.

- **Encourage Budgeting and Tracking Spending**

  Once your kids are old enough, encourage them to create a basic budget for their allowance or any earnings they may receive. Help them track their spending to show the impact of their decisions. This practice builds awareness and accountability for managing money.

- **Teach the Principles of Giving Back**

  Show your kids that money isn't just for personal gain, it's a way to create positive change in the world. Encourage them to allocate a portion of their earnings to a cause they care about. This reinforces the value of generosity as a pillar of your family's financial legacy.

- **Model Responsible Financial Behavior**

  Kids learn by watching the adults in their lives. Demonstrate sound financial habits, prioritize saving, live within your means, and talk openly about budgeting or financial challenges. Transparency helps demystify money and makes it easier for children to ask questions.

Building Future Stewards

It's not enough to educate kids about finances; you must also foster a mindset of stewardship. Encourage them to see family wealth as more than a resource to spend, it's a legacy to protect, nurture, and grow. Insights from *Legally Ever After* emphasize that the most successful families treat wealth as a tool to achieve long-term goals, sustain values, and create opportunities. When children inherit this mindset, they carry forward not just the money, but the purpose behind it.

- **Create a Family Constitution or Mission Statement**

  A formal statement about your family's values, goals, and approach to wealth can provide guidance for future generations. This document serves as a compass, helping children and grandchildren make decisions that align with the family's vision.

- **Organize Financial Planning Meetings**

  Hold regular meetings where your family openly discusses the state of wealth, its goals, and the steps being taken to achieve those goals. This practice normalizes financial conversations and ensures that everyone feels involved in the process.

- **Mentor Them Through Hands-On Experience**

  Give your children opportunities to make financial decisions, such as managing part of an inheritance through a trust or taking responsibility for a family business project. These experiences serve as invaluable lessons in accountability and leadership.

Strengthening the Foundation

Teaching your kids to become stewards of generational wealth requires a thoughtful combination of education, experience, and shared purpose. It's about preparing them not just to manage money but to carry forward the values, goals, and dreams that your family holds dear. You're equipping them to face financial challenges with clarity, grow wealth sustainably, and use it as a force for good in their lives and the lives of others.

By investing in their financial literacy and stewardship skills today, you're ensuring that your legacy thrives, generation after generation. Wealth isn't just a gift for your children, it's a responsibility, and with the right tools, they'll be ready to honor it. Start planting these seeds of knowledge now, and watch your legacy flourish.

APPENDIX E: WEDDING
BUDGET SECRETS

HOW WE HAD A DREAM WEDDING
WITHOUT BREAKING THE BANK

If you're planning a wedding, or any big event, you don't have to spend a fortune to make it special. Here are six budget-friendly wedding strategies that saved us thousands of dollars while still creating an incredible experience:

1. **Opted for a YMCA Wedding**
   » Instead of an expensive venue, we booked a *YMCA lodge in the mountains*, which had breathtaking views at a fraction of the cost.

2. **Brought in Our Own Alcohol**
   » Many venues charge outrageous prices for alcohol. We brought our own and *only paid for what we used*, returning the rest.

3. **Food Truck Rehearsal Dinner**
   » Instead of a costly restaurant dinner, we had a food truck at a scenic lake park, giving us a unique and affordable experience.

4. **Repurposed Ceremony Flowers for the Reception**
   - » Instead of buying double the flowers, we moved the arrangements from the ceremony to the reception.

5. **Hired a Day-of Wedding Coordinator**
   - » We skipped an expensive full-service planner and hired a coordinator just for the day to help with setup and takedown.

6. **Donated My Dress and Flowers for a Tax Write-Off**
   - » After the wedding, I donated my wedding dress and floral arrangements to charities, which provided a valuable tax deduction.

By sticking to our budget and making intentional choices, we started our marriage without financial stress - and were able to buy our first home!

APPENDIX F: MASTERING CREDIT

A COMPLETE GUIDE TO BUILDING, PROTECTING, AND TEACHING FINANCIAL SUCCESS FOR YOU AND YOUR CHILDREN

Starting my business came with an unexpected twist. My original plan was to use a bonus from my employer to get things off the ground, but when that fell through, I turned to a zero-percent interest credit card to make it happen. It wasn't what I had planned, but it taught me a valuable lesson about the power and pitfalls of credit. Credit cards can be effective tools when used responsibly but also carry risks. In this section, we will explore why improving your credit score matters and practical steps you can take to build or repair it.

Why Good Credit is Important

Maintaining good credit can greatly simplify your life and help you save significant money over time. Consider your credit score as a grade that indicates your trustworthiness in managing finances. The higher your "grade," the more opportunities you will have.

Benefits of Good Credit

Good credit can open a world of benefits that make everyday life easier and less stressful. Here are a few ways it can help:

- **Lower Interest Rates on Loans and Credit Cards**

  Imagine borrowing money to purchase a car. With good credit, the bank may charge you a lower interest rate, which means you'll pay them less over time. For instance, paying 3% interest instead of 10% could save you hundreds or even thousands of dollars!

- **Easier Approval for Loans and Credit Cards**

  Want a credit card to earn rewards or need a loan for a house? Good credit boosts your chances of approval. Lenders see you as trustworthy, which makes them more inclined to work with you.

- **Better Rental Opportunities**

  Many landlords check your credit before renting an apartment. If they see that you have good credit, they're more likely to accept your application. Additionally, with good credit, you probably won't need to pay a large deposit to set up services like electricity or internet in your new home.

- **Favorable Terms on Insurance and Jobs**

  Believe it or not, some companies consider your credit history when determining car insurance rates or even when hiring for a job. Good credit reflects your responsibility, which can result in lower insurance costs or help you land that dream job.

Long-term Financial Advantages

Good credit isn't just about getting approved for things in the moment; it also lays a foundation for long-term success. Here's how:

- **Saving Money Over Time**

  Lower interest rates on items such as mortgages, car loans, and credit cards mean you'll pay less to borrow the same amount. For example, if you take out a $200,000 mortgage, having good credit could save you *tens of thousands of dollars* in interest over 30 years. That's money you could allocate towards a vacation, college savings, or retirement!

- **Flexibility in Emergencies**

  Life happens. Whether it's an unexpected car repair or a medical bill, good credit can help you secure a loan quickly when needed. It serves as a safety net just in case.

How Credit is Ranked

Your credit score serves as a report card for your finances. It indicates to lenders how likely you are to repay borrowed money. A good score signifies that you are deemed trustworthy, whereas a lower score may present challenges. Let's break it down to understand how credit is ranked in the U.S.

Understanding the U.S. Credit Score Range (300–850)

Credit scores in the U.S. range from 300 to 850, like a grading scale. The higher your score, the more lenders will trust you. If you're at the top of the scale, banks and credit card companies see you as someone who pays back debts on time and manages credit responsibly. Conversely, a lower score may lead lenders to view you as a higher risk for lending money.

Lenders, including banks and landlords, take this score into account when determining whether to approve applications for loans, credit cards, or even rental agreements for apartments.

Credit Score Categories

Here's how the scores are organized and what they signify for you:

- **300–579 (Poor)**

  This is akin to receiving an "F" in school. With this score, you may find it extremely difficult to be approved for loans or credit cards. If you do qualify, you will likely face very high interest rates.

- **580–669 (Fair)**

  This is like a "C" grade. You can receive credit, but the options might come with high fees or less favorable terms.

- **670–739 (Good)**

  A "B" grade! Most lenders view you as reliable, and you're likely to get approved for various loans or credit cards with reasonable interest rates.

- **740–799 (Very Good)**

  An "A" for financial trustworthiness! With this score, you'll enjoy better deals, such as lower interest rates and favorable terms.

- **800–850 (Exceptional)**

  You're a straight-A student in the world of credit! Achieving this score unlocks the best rates and benefits, ultimately saving you the most money over time.

FACTORS THAT INFLUENCE YOUR CREDIT SCORE

Five key factors influence your credit score. Understanding these factors enables you to identify what to focus on to improve or maintain your score:

1. Payment History (35% of your score)

Paying bills on time is the most important factor. Think of it as turning in homework punctually. If you're consistently late, your grade (or in this case, your score) drops. Even one missed payment can have a negative impact!

Paying your credit card bill late could not only lower your score but may also result in negative consequences in the form of late fees.

2. Credit Utilization (30%)

This measures the amount of your available credit that you're currently using. Lenders prefer to see a low percentage. For instance, if you have a $1,000 credit limit and utilize $300, your utilization rate is 30%, which is favorable. Conversely, if you max out your card and owe $1,000, that's 100%, and it could negatively impact your score.

3. Length of Credit History (15%)

The longer you use credit, the better it is. It shows lenders that you have experience managing money wisely.

Pro Tip: Keeping older accounts, even if they aren't used often, can help increase your credit age.

4. Credit Mix (10%)

Having a variety of credit types is advantageous. For example, a blend of a credit card, car loan, and student loan showcases your ability to manage different forms of credit responsibly.

5. New Credit Inquiries (10%)

Each time you apply for new credit, it results in a "hard inquiry," which can temporarily reduce your score. Applying for too many accounts in a short period, such as multiple credit cards, may make lenders concerned that you're relying excessively on borrowed funds.

A QUICK RECAP

Your credit is essentially your financial reputation. It's ranked on a scale from 300 to 850, with higher scores unlocking better opportunities and savings. By understanding what goes into your score and taking small steps to improve it, you can keep climbing toward credit success.

Practical Recommendations to Improve Your Credit

Improving your credit score doesn't have to be complicated. With a few good habits and simple steps, you can watch your credit score grow over time. Here's how to take control of your credit and set yourself up for financial success.

1. Review and Understand Your Credit Report

Your credit report is a comprehensive record of your borrowing history, and it's important to understand what's contained within it. You can obtain a free copy from AnnualCreditReport.com once a year. Examine it carefully for errors such as incorrect balances or duplicate accounts. If you notice any discrepancies, you can dispute them and have them corrected.

If your report indicates a credit card balance that you have already paid off, correcting that mistake can swiftly enhance your score.

2. Pay Bills on Time

This is the golden rule of good credit: paying your bills on time shows lenders that you are reliable. If you have trouble remembering due dates, consider using budgeting apps.

Tip: Just one late payment can damage your score, so set reminders to keep yourself on schedule.

3. Reduce Credit Card Balances

Maintaining low credit card balances is another effective strategy for building your score. Experts suggest using less than 30% of your credit limit, while striving for under 10% is even more advantageous.

If you have several balances, consider using one of these strategies to pay them off:

- Avalanche Method: Pay off the debts with the highest interest rates first to save more money over time.
- Snowball Method: Begin with your smallest debt to achieve an easy win, then progress to larger ones.

Example: If your credit card limit is $1,000, aim to maintain your balance under $300. This demonstrates to lenders that you can manage your spending responsibly.

4. Manage Credit Utilization

If your credit utilization is too high, you can request a credit limit increase from your credit card company. This doesn't mean you should spend more, but it can help lower the percentage of credit being used. Additionally, check your balances regularly to ensure you're on track.

Example: If your limit increases from $1,000 to $2,000 and you're still only using $300, your credit utilization decreases from 30% to 15%, which is beneficial for your score!

5. Keep Old Accounts Open

Older credit accounts enhance your overall credit history, which lenders appreciate. Even if you no longer use an old credit card, keeping it open can benefit your score. Just ensure it doesn't have annual fees or other charges.

Consider your old credit account a trophy from the past. It demonstrates to lenders that you've been responsible for years, instilling confidence in them about you.

6. Limit Hard Credit Checks

Every time you apply for a new credit card or loan, lenders perform a "hard inquiry," which can slightly affect your score. Multiple inquiries within a short period may lead lenders to believe you're desperate for credit. Only apply when you truly need it and try to consolidate several applications (for a car or home loan, for example) into a brief timeframe so they count as a single inquiry.

Example: If you're exploring options for a new car loan, apply with several lenders within the same week instead of extending your applications over months.

Start Building Better Credit Today

Improving your credit is all about taking small, steady steps. By following these tips, you can get closer to your financial goals and enjoy the benefits of having a strong credit score. It's like planting a garden, with a little care and patience, you'll watch it grow into something amazing!

How to Establish Good Credit for Your Kids

- **Add Children as Authorized Users**
  - » Help them establish credit via the positive history of your credit card accounts.
  - » Warning: If your credit score isn't high enough, avoid adding your children as authorized users. A low credit score or poor payment history can negatively impact their credit instead of helping them.
- **Choose the Right Card**
  - » Use a card with a long, clean payment history and low balances.
  - » Avoid cards with high fees or poor terms.
- **Teach Financial Responsibility**
  - » Set clear boundaries (spending caps, no physical card if necessary).
  - » Monitor statements and ensure they align with agreed-upon behaviors.
- **Benefits for Kids**
  - » Early credit-building offers future benefits, such as easier loan approvals and rental applications.
  - » Learning good habits early fosters financial independence.

When to Freeze Your Credit and How to Do It

Freezing your credit may seem drastic, but at times, it's the most effective way to safeguard yourself against fraud. Consider it akin to locking your front door to keep intruders away. Here's a guide on when to freeze your credit, why it's beneficial, and how to do it.

When Freezing Credit is Necessary

Freezing your credit can be a wise decision in certain situations. Here are the key times to consider doing so:

- **After a Major Data Breach**

  Recent incidents, such as the National Public Data breach, which exposed sensitive information from approximately 1.3 million records, along with larger leaks like the Change Healthcare and AT&T breaches, demonstrate how stolen data frequently ends up on the dark web, where it can be sold or resold indefinitely. Freezing your credit prevents this data from being used to open fraudulent accounts in your name.

- **When Identity Theft is Suspected or Confirmed**

  If you notice strange charges on your accounts or get calls about loans you didn't apply for, it's a red flag. Freezing your credit can help you take control while fixing the problem.

- **If You're Not Applying for Credit Right Now**

  If you're not planning to take out a loan or sign up for a credit card anytime soon, freezing your credit adds an extra layer of protection against fraud. It's particularly helpful if you simply want peace of mind.

Benefits of Freezing Credit

Here's why freezing your credit is a good idea in certain situations:

- **It Blocks Thieves from Opening New Accounts**

  If someone tries to use your stolen information to get a credit card or loan, they will be denied because your credit report will be locked.

- **It Provides Peace of Mind**

  Knowing your credit is secure can enhance your sleep, particularly during instances of significant personal data breaches or if you've been targeted by scammers.

How to Freeze Your Credit

Freezing your credit is quick and straightforward. Here's how you can do it:

1. **Contact the Three Major Credit Bureaus**

   Reach out to Experian, Equifax, and TransUnion. You can do this online or by phone.

2. **Provide Documentation**

   Be ready to share information like your Social Security number and a copy of your ID to verify your identity.

3. **Obtain a PIN or Password**

   When you freeze your credit, you will receive a unique PIN or password. This is necessary to temporarily lift the freeze if you choose to apply for credit later.

4. **It's Now Free**

   Thanks to federal rules, freezing your credit doesn't cost a dime.

ABOUT THE AUTHOR

Pamela Maass Garrett (aka Law Mother®) is an estate planning attorney, entrepreneur, and wealth strategist on a mission to help families and business owners build, protect, and pass down generational wealth. As the founder of **Law Mother®,** she has helped thousands of families create financial security and lasting legacies, avoiding the confusion and the sense of being overwhelmed that usually comes with money and legal planning.

But Pamela's expertise isn't just professional, it's personal. She started her law firm in 2019 with a **0% interest credit card,** built it into a *seven-figure business*, and did it all while navigating new motherhood and the financial uncertainty of a global pandemic. She discovered the same proven wealth-building strategies that high-net-worth families use to **grow, multiply, and protect their money**. Now, she's sharing those strategies with you.

Pamela has been featured on The Drew Barrymore Show and built a thriving online community of over 2.8 million social media followers by making financial education simple, engaging, and, dare we say, fun. When she's not helping families achieve their Wealthy Ever After, she's a dedicated mom, business owner, and advocate for financial empowerment.

www.ingramcontent.com/pod-product-compliance
Lightning Source LLC
Chambersburg PA
CBHW071558210326
41597CB00019B/3295